REINVENTING CHEESECAKE

Written by Jaime Firbank

Produced by designbygary.co.uk

Images by Gary and Adam

designbygary.co.uk & adamgallifordphotography.co.uk

© Copyright
My Sweet Publications 2021
All rights reserved.

The content contained within this book may not be reproduced, duplicated or transmitted without direct permission from the author or publisher.

DEDICATED TO ROB AND LORRAINE FIRBANK

How to get the most out of this book

I've made the book simple and easy to follow but, sometimes I find I learn more quickly from watching someone demonstrate something, so I've made short videos to help you along your cheesecake-making journey, I highly recommend watching the videos.

Simply scan the QR code, or go to cheesecakegeek.com

As well as exclusive access to all the videos, you'll receive additional recipes:

Bonus 1: My perfect brownies
Bonus 2: Blondies to die for
Bonus 3: Delicious Cookie dough
Bonus 4: Amazing Hokey Pokey
Bonus 5: My 2-minute Keto cheesecake

You'll find lots of help and advice and also meet new friends in my Facebook group, Cheesecake Geek World.

CONTENTS

2	Introduction and how the obsession started
9	I want to teach you how to think like a cook and not just follow recipes

What you'll need

12	Cheesecake's basic ingredients
14	The equipment

Methods

18	The biscuit or crumb base
21	The pie effect
24	The standard cheesecake baking methods
26	Project: 'Make the perfect cheesecake mix so I can add any additional flavors and easily make any and every cheesecake I'd ever need to'
28	The Eureka moment!
30	The 'Secret baking method'
34	Special Effects
35	Spectacular layers
35	The marble effect
36	The zebra stripe
38	Adding donuts/cookies/brownies etc
40	Mini chocolate piping bag
41	Removing the cheesecake from the tin
42	Chocolate ganache drip
46	Decorating a spectacular cheesecake
50	Customizing the donuts

Recipes

55	Biscoff
57	Strawberries and Cream Baileys
59	Kinder Madness
61	New York-style
63	The Salted Caramel dip
65	Cherry Nutella brownie
67	Blueberry swirl
69	Key Lime
73	Banoffee Pie
75	The Oreo
77	Reese's Peanut Butter Cup
79	Cookie dough
81	Chocolate Fudge brownie
83	White chocolate Krispy Kreme
85	Netflix and Chilll'd
87	The Incredible Oreo and Biscoff swirl
89	Chocolate Mint
91	Your recipe!
92	Conclusion

INTRODUCTION AND HOW THE OBSESSION STARTED

"Hey, Jaime! Have you entered the Bake Off?"

"The what?" I replied.

People kept asking me the same question all day, "Have you entered? You should enter the Doncaster Bake Off with your cheesecakes, you'll win."

"Hmm, I don't know," I said, "I'm sure there will be plenty of professional bakers there, with some amazing cakes. There's no point, I wouldn't stand a chance."

So, I entered the Doncaster Bake Off back in 2017, and amazingly I won first prize with a Cherry Bakewell cheesecake. This was when I realized it was time to go all-in, take the leap, and set up my own business. I knew my cakes had to look impressive to stand out from any others. I needed my own unique style, which had to be eye-catching as well as delicious.

I've always loved cooking. I remember being fascinated by how flour, butter, and eggs could transform into soft fluffy, delicious sponge cake when my dad taught my sister and me how to bake cupcakes. My dad was the cook in the house, although occasionally, my mum would try something. We would usually have the emergency services on standby, just in case, and then tell the neighbors to evacuate their houses until it was over.

I started making my own lunch and dinners at about 9-years old, watching my dad make them and then wanting to do so myself. I realized food was supposed to not only taste wonderful but should also look appealing when I created animals and faces with the food on my plate.

I always wanted my own business but never knew what to do. Cheesecakes would never have entered my mind, particularly as I think I'd only ever made one before in primary school when I was about seven.
I learned how to make restaurant-style Indian food from an eBook I found online and immediately started making curries, rice, and naan bread. My work colleagues kept asking me to make for them too. It started as just one or two, and before I knew it, I was spending all day Sunday making curries, rice, and naan bread and then taking them to work on the Monday. I worked in a large call center, so word got around quickly.

I loved making them, but after five hours of cooking, there was a lot of mess to clean up. Somehow, I'am able to make a mess with spectacular ease.

After a couple of years of making curries, I wanted to try something different, and that would take less cleaning up. I liked the idea of making desserts. I could use my artistic side, making them look and taste delicious.

> I KNEW MY CAKES HAD TO LOOK IMPRESSIVE TO STAND OUT FROM ANY OTHERS

I had seen some delectable-looking Belgian waffles on Instagram that had every type of topping. I'd never eaten one before, never mind trying to make one. With absolutely no experience, I decided to email all my work colleagues and told them, "Next week I'm making Belgian waffles, who would like some?" Within 30 mins I had orders for 90 waffles!

"I had better order that waffle iron from Amazon" I thought, "and learn how to make them pretty quickly."

Whatever I make, I want it to be the absolute best. Restaurant-quality is the goal!

I always ask everyone, "Would you be happy if you bought this in a restaurant?"

Whether it's a curry, a Belgian waffle, a pizza, or a cheesecake, it must be the best you can make at home.

Almost a year later, someone said "Why don't you start making cheesecakes? Everyone loves cheesecakes."

..... That's when the obsession started.

I remember the first one I ever attempted was the Vanilla Bean Cheesecake from the Cheesecake Factory. It was a layer of vanilla cheesecake with a top layer of white chocolate mousse (which I'd never made before either). After two days of work, the masterpiece was finally ready. I took a step back, about to admire its beauty and to wallow in pride at what my hard work and skill had produced.

Slowly the expectation of cheesecake perfection diminished. The reality came crashing down on me. "This is not as easy as it looks," I thought. The more I gazed upon the unstable-looking structure in front of me, all I could think was that it looked like a 5-year-old had made it, with his patient and proud mum looking on. I took it to work anyway, and they all loved it.

From that moment on, my cheesecake love affair started, not only with me but also with my work colleagues. I started selling them by the slice at first. I'd tell everyone what flavors I was going to make for the following week, and by Friday, all the slices had been pre-ordered. "I love them, they're so creamy", someone said, "What do you put in them?" "Cream," I replied with a big smile on my face.

I worked with about 800 people in the call center at that stage. It was the perfect testing ground for my recipes, and I could get feedback from everyone. If they were too sweet, too thick, not enough flavor, I was sure to be told. I could also ask everyone what they liked about each cheesecake and what could be improved.

I knew I was onto something. Everyone was telling me that these were the best cheesecake they had ever eaten. I knew, however, the cakes needed something more, something to make them stand out. I had to have my individual style of decoration. I saw people online decorating cakes with several types of chocolate bars and sweets.

I realized I had to make mine look decadent and excel with the toppings. They were an instant success. Two years later I left work and started my own business. I had already thought of the name Cheesecake Geek. When I was making the curries while working in the call center, I had thought of the name Curry Geek, so Cheesecake Geek was the obvious choice.

I experimented with about five different cheesecake recipes until I was able to create my own unique version, taking elements from each one. I didn't want my cheesecake to be too dense, but somewhere between baked and non-baked. I had to ensure my final recipe was thick enough to hold its shape under the weight of various toppings, be rich and creamy but not overly sweet.

I discovered most recipes contained large amounts of sugar, so I reduced the sugar content by almost half. I could only think this amount of sugar was to compete with the sour cream. "If you use less sugar," I thought, "and replace it with double/heavy cream, then it won't need as much sugar." I was right.

> FROM THAT MOMENT ON, MY CHEESECAKE LOVE AFFAIR STARTED

The biscuit base had to be thick, crunchy, and buttery, and the ratio to cheesecake had to be balanced. About 4:1 seemed the perfect proportion.

Also, with my final version, I could add any other flavors and ingredients to the mix without adjusting the recipe. This meant I could make big batches of the original cheesecake at the beginning of the day and add the different ingredients to each individual cheesecake to change the flavor as and when I needed to.

The ultimate act of kindness

In this electronic age we live in, physically making something for someone or for a special occasion, is the ultimate way to show you care. Baking a cake for someone either as a gift, an "I love you", congratulations, a get well soon or just a simple thank you, is a wonderful way to show how much you appreciate them.

You've taken the time, and you've created something unique just for them (and you, if they give you a slice, that is). Then they can share it with others and so increase the 'love' even more (aww).

And with your showstopping cheesecakes, it's something they'll never forget.

WHITE CHOCOLATE KRISPY KREME

I WANT TO TEACH YOU HOW TO THINK LIKE A COOK AND NOT JUST FOLLOW RECIPES

The goal of this book is for you to recreate the Cheesecake Geek style cheesecakes. Not only that, I want you to create your personal, unique flavor combinations and designs.

What's wonderful about cheesecakes is they are a blank canvas. You can create almost any flavor, sweet, salty, chocolaty, fruity. I'll be breaking down every stage of the process in detail, so the first cheesecake you create from the book will be the best one you've ever created.

I'll be giving examples of alternative ingredients throughout the book. Feel free to change the milk chocolate to white, replace the brownies with blondies or the cherry flavor with raspberry, and add color to them, creating beautiful marbling effects. As you progress, you'll also create your style. Your family and friends will be amazed and will want you to make beautiful cheesecakes for every and any event from then on (and your family will probably start expecting you to).

The secret baking method I'm teaching you is the one I created myself, after four years and 100's of cheesecakes.

The idea came to me when I was thinking about how I could stop the donuts from rising to the top of the cake during baking. As soon as the cheesecake mix got up to temperature in the oven, they would just float to the top. This was frustrating, as I wanted them to sit in the middle so when I sliced the cake, you could see the donut's perfect profile.

I'd done this successfully with no-bake cheesecakes, but my passion is baked cheesecake. I'd never seen anyone who had done it before, but I couldn't stop thinking that there had to be a way.

After several attempts, I got it to work. Now I can add almost anything I can think of, and it won't melt, or dissolve, and it will keep its shape perfectly.

WHAT YOU'LL NEED

CHEESECAKE'S BASIC INGREDIENTS

The cream cheese

Only use full-fat cream cheese. Most brands vary from 25% to 35% fat content. Philadelphia is probably the most famous brand but can be more expensive. I've experimented with several good supermarket own-name brands, and I found they were equally as good, thick, creamy, and tangy.

As a guideline, the ones with the least amount of 'whey' (the water that separates from the cheese and collects on top of it) usually tend to be the better ones.

The biscuit/cookie/crumb base

Whatever you choose to call it, many people have told me this is their favorite part of the cheesecake, crunchy and buttery, as it's the perfect complement to the thick and creamy cheese. You can use any biscuits or cookies of your choice. The amount of butter will depend on your choice of biscuit. Some biscuits have a higher butter content or have a creme filling, so need less butter, and others are dryer, so may need more.

'Digestives' are the most traditional biscuits (cookies) used for the base in the UK. These are the closest to the traditional U.S. cheesecake cookie base, 'Graham' crackers. They have different flavors but are similar in texture. Ginger biscuits are called ginger snaps (makes sense). My favorite biscuit of all is the mind-blowing Lotus Biscoff, also known as Speculoos in some parts of the world.

Gluten-free?

Simple, just use gluten-free biscuits/cookies. There are plenty on the market today.

Butter

I use salted butter as I find it adds more flavor. As long as it's real butter, you can use any.

Cream

Double cream or heavy whipping cream has approximately 48% fat content, which is needed to produce the wonderful thick creaminess of the finished cake.

Eggs

Eggs are essential for making your cheesecake set. Make sure they are as fresh as possible.

Three medium eggs work perfectly for the recipes. For a slightly creamier mix, I add two additional yolks, particularly to the New York-style recipe.

Always crack them into a separate jug or bowl first, never directly into the cheesecake mix. It's much easier to fish out any stray pieces of shell that way.

Flour

Use plain or all-purpose flour. (Don't use self-raising flour as I did once, accidentally).

Gluten-free?

Easy modification again, just replace the flour with two tablespoons of cornflour, done!!

Sugar

Granulated white sugar is the standard, but you could just as easily use brown or any other type. Be aware, though, that a different sugar may change the consistency slightly, and brown sugar isn't quite as sweet as the white stuff.

Sugar alternatives

You can even go sugar-free by swapping the sugar for Stevia, Erythritol, honey, or your favorite sweetener. The sugar alternatives do have different levels of sweetness, so you can adjust the amounts to your liking.

Vanilla

Vanilla can make the difference between a mediocre and a delicious cheesecake. There are numerous artificial vanilla flavorings on the market, and they just taste nasty and synthetic, leaving a weird chemical aftertaste. We were raised to almost believe vanilla is a non-flavor and the "plain" option, but good quality vanilla adds a warm sweet note to anything and even enhances other flavors.

Although it costs more, you only ever use a small amount for each cake, so it will last a while, and it will make your cakes stand out from others.

Food coloring

I use the concentrated drops for the cheesecakes. They are easier and less messy to use than the gel/paste, although the gel/paste is perfectly fine too. For coloring white chocolate ganache, use a gel/paste. If you use drops, be careful not to add too much liquid, or it will have trouble setting.

Extracts

It's worth paying a bit more for decent quality extracts, as they will last a while, and most supermarkets have their own high-end name brand. Check the label to make sure they contain the natural oils.

Using scales rather than cups.

I'm not going to go on about how much better digital scales are than using cups. Yes, digital scales are more accurate, and I would always recommend using them. They are inexpensive, and you will probably start using them for everything you cook.

I'll be using grams throughout the book, however, unlike a traditionally baked cheesecake which can crack easily with just the slightest indiscretion, my secret baking method is very forgiving and allows for adjustments with the ingredients.

I've made so many cheesecakes, I rarely use my scales anymore, if I'm a few grams out occasionally it doesn't make any noticeable difference.

THE EQUIPMENT

You don't need vast quantities of kitchen tools and gadgets, but certain items are essential:

9" silicone or metal springform cake tin

I started using the glass-bottomed silicone springform cake tins some years ago (it is neither a springform nor a tin (?), but never mind). I would certainly recommend getting one. They guarantee nothing will stick to the inside of the tin, giving you smoother sides to the cheesecake, and it makes removing the cake much easier. You can easily find the silicone 'springforms' online.

Don't worry if you can't find a 9" tin. If you have an 8" one, it won't make much difference. You can use different size cake tins, as you will see, but the standard recipe fits snugly into a 9" one.

Ovenproof bowl 5 liter/5 quart

I use a 5-liter glass bowl to bake the cheesecake in the oven, but the classic ceramic bowls work just as well.

Silicone spatula

These things are incredible. If you've never used one before, you'll wonder how you've coped all this time. There is no wastage and an easier clean-up afterwards.

A large mixing bowl, 5 liter/5 quart

This can be glass or plastic for mixing additional ingredients into the cheesecake mix.

1 Litre measuring jug

Perfect for the ganache and mixing small amounts of cheesecake mix with assorted flavors and colors.

Digital scales, measuring cups

I've included cups and spoons into the measurements, although digital scales are an incredibly useful kitchen gadget and are more accurate than cups. Plus, you will save on cleaning the different size cups.

Flat bottom and side glass/mug

This is to make the biscuit base neat and even, and you need the straight sides when making the pie effect.

Food processor or rolling pin and sealable food bag

Food processors can make cooking much easier, and they can save time, especially when used for breaking the biscuits down to crumbs for the base, although they are not essential. A simple sealable food bag and a good old rolling pin will do the trick.

Electric stand or hand mixer

If you've ever whisked a bowl of double/heavy cream before and had your arms feel like they're going to fall off, you know the huge advantage of a hand mixer. Don't think you have to go out and buy one. But if you want to use your muscle power, and have a mini arm workout, that's fine.

Zester or fine cheese grater

The long-handled ones are best and sturdier when zesting citrus fruit. Remember to use only unwaxed fruit. Check the labels first before buying to see if the fruit is unwaxed.

Turntable

Do you need one? No, but when it comes to decorating your cheesecake, turntables make things much easier. It will also double as an attractive cake stand.

Sandwich bags for piping

Small sandwich bags from most supermarkets work perfectly well as mini piping bags. We'll be using these for sticking the cheesecake to the cake board and decorating the donuts.

Sharp carving knife

You've made a fantastic cheesecake, and you want to present a beautiful slice to everyone. Don't ruin it by hacking into the cheesecake like a crazed lumberjack.

You'll need a long (6-7") sharp straight-edge knife, preferably long and thin, a jug of boiling water, and some kitchen roll.

Carefully move aside any donuts or chocolate. Place the knife in the boiling water for a few seconds, wipe the excess water away, and starting from the center of the cake, cut down on a slight angle (knife pointing down).

Repeat the process for every slice; hot water, wipe knife, slice, water, wipe, slice…

Prepare everything before you start

Although I've tried to make everything as foolproof as possible, there's nothing worse than getting halfway through a recipe and then realizing you've forgotten something (usually a key ingredient) or misread part of the method.

Read through the method, have the equipment close to hand, and have all the ingredients weighed, the cream cheese, eggs, and cream at room temperature (so they mix together easily).

METHODS

THE BISCUIT OR CRUMB BASE

Just so we're all clear and on the same page - cookies are biscuits, and biscuits are cookies.

In the UK, the only thing we refer to as a cookie is chocolate chip cookies. Everything else, as far as we're concerned, is a biscuit. We dunk them lovingly into our cup of tea or coffee.

Different biscuits have different ingredients and therefore need different amounts of butter. The ones with creme in the middle (like Oreos) don't need as much. Because all biscuit brands vary slightly, it's best to add less butter at the start, as you can always add a little more if needed.

The perfect mixture should have the consistency of wet sand. When you squeeze a small handful, it should hold itself together easily, without crumbling apart.

Please note that ginger and Biscoff biscuits tend to dissolve in the warm butter and become too wet, so for a 350g mix, use 200g Digestive/Graham and 150g Biscoff or ginger. Don't worry, the strong flavors of the biscuits will still come through.

For a cheesecake pie, you'll need an extra 250g of biscuit mix to go up the sides of the tin, and just add the additional butter needed.

A basic guideline for 350g biscuits

Digestives/Graham = 100g

Oreo's = 65g

Ginger mix = 80g

Biscoff mix = 60g

Bourbon (a chocolate biscuit with chocolate creme) = 60g

Method

We'll be using Digestives/Graham crackers.

Melt 100g butter in a saucepan over low heat, or in the microwave in short bursts. Put 350g Digestives/Graham crackers in a food processor, or smash them in a sealed food bag with a rolling pin.

Pour the melted butter into the crumbs (if you're using a tin, leave a small amount for greasing the tin) and mix it evenly together, ensuring no big lumps are remaining.

Tip the biscuit mix into the tin, spread it evenly with the spatula, and then press down gently at first with the bottom of the glass or mug, gradually applying a little more pressure every time. As you do this, turn the cake tin, and look at it from each side to ensure the base is even.

Finally, using a spoon, run it around the sides of the biscuit base leveling the edge to get an even base.

Use the remaining butter to grease the sides of the tin (no need to do this if you're using silicone) to prevent the cheesecake from sticking, and pop it into the freezer until you're ready to use it.

I've experimented with baking the base before using it, and I blind-tested my family with both a baked and non-baked base. They couldn't tell the difference.

THE PIE EFFECT

First, make the standard base. For the sides of the crust, you'll need an extra 250g of biscuit crumbs and the equivalent amount of butter.

Pour this into the tin and carefully build the walls by pressing the biscuit up the sides of the tin, making it an even thickness all around.

Once you're happy with it, use the mug or glass to gently compact the newly constructed crunchy, buttery walls of awesomeness.

Place it in the freezer (while you bake the cheesecake mix), so the biscuit hardens. You don't want any of it to fall apart and have to make unnecessary repairs later.

To be creative and for an even bigger wow factor, make separate smaller mixes of two or more different biscuits bases and add them in separate piles in the cake tin before spreading them out.

Your guests will be able to see the different colors clearly and taste the different biscuits as they devour your latest masterpiece.

Oreo and Biscoff work well together.

CHERRY NUTELLA BROWNIE

THE STANDARD CHEESECAKE BAKING METHODS

In my quest for the perfect cheesecake, I experimented with numerous different methods, temperatures, and baking times. Each one had advantages and disadvantages.

To test when the cheesecake is ready with all these methods, it will have a slight 'jiggle in the middle'. The edges will look firm, and only the center will move if you shake the tin slightly. This is exactly how you want it, so don't be tempted to keep cooking it.

The cheesecake mix will continue to bake for 30 minutes after cooking. Open the oven door slightly and turn the oven off. The cheesecake can cool slowly this way, and it will help prevent your beautiful cake from cracking.

None of these methods is perfect, and I've had cakes crack on me using all these methods.

Just bake it

Advantages: Simple.

Disadvantages: Most likely method for it to crack.

The simplest method is to place the cheesecake in the middle of the oven and bake it 'low and slow'.

A water bath

Advantages: Much less likely to crack, smooth and creamy texture

Disadvantages: If you have any holes in the foil, the water will leak in, destroying the biscuit base, and there is the risk of spilling hot water everywhere.

You'll need a deep baking tray with an inch of water in it. Seal the cake tin with two layers of aluminum foil all the way around the outside, and carefully place it in the water bath.

Not only does this keep the cheesecake temperature consistent during baking, but it keeps the air humid and the temperature consistent in the oven, which helps with 'hot spots'.

This is definitely the best method of the three, but there's always a chance some water will find its way into the tin. It can also produce too much steam in the oven, so the water droplets will fall onto your cheesecake.

A cup or tray of water

Advantages: Easier than the water bath.

Disadvantages: Still may crack if the cake cooks too fast.

Place a mug or tray of water in the oven to create steam in the oven to keep the temperature consistent without the need for a water bath.

It definitely helps, but when it comes to getting the perfect baked cheesecake, it's still culinary Russian roulette, though.

PROJECT: 'MAKE THE PERFECT CHEESECAKE MIX SO I CAN ADD ANY ADDITIONAL FLAVORS AND EASILY MAKE ANY AND EVERY CHEESECAKE I'D EVER NEED TO'

The 'secret' cheesecake mix

This will be the only cheesecake mix you'll ever need. I've seen so many questions on Facebook and have been asked, "Do you have a recipe for a chocolate cheesecake or a Biscoff or lemon, etc?"

I wondered why there were so many different recipes. If you had the perfect vanilla recipe, why not just use that and add in any other flavors?

It had to be simpler than having a different recipe for every cheesecake. If I needed to be making ten cheesecakes a day, I had to have a base mix that I could make in bulk and add whatever I wanted to it to change the flavor and make it a completely different cheesecake.

So began, Project: 'Make the perfect cheesecake mix so I can add any additional flavors and make any and every cheesecake I ever needed to'.

It worked perfectly, and I could now make a big batch up of the newly named 'secret cheesecake base mix' (which was confused with the base mix, also known as the biscuit base or crust mix).

So, I renamed it the 'Secret Cheesecake Mix'.

Ingredients

1200g full-fat cream cheese (room temperature)

65g plain/all-purpose flour

150g sugar

1Tbsp vanilla extract or paste (I like using the paste as you see the tiny vanilla seeds in the cheesecake)

300ml heavy/double cream

3 large eggs

Method

Preheat the oven to 160C/320F

Add the cream cheese, sugar, flour, vanilla to the mixing bowl, and mix them together by hand or with an electric mixer, until everything is just combined.

Crack the eggs into a jug to prevent any rogue shell pieces escaping into the mix. You don't want your guests' munching on eggshells. Beat them together.

Now add the egg to the cream cheese mix.

Fold the beaten eggs into the mixture until they have disappeared.

Add the cream and mix until everything is thoroughly combined.

Boom!

This is now YOUR 'Secret Cheesecake Mix'.

THE EUREKA MOMENT!

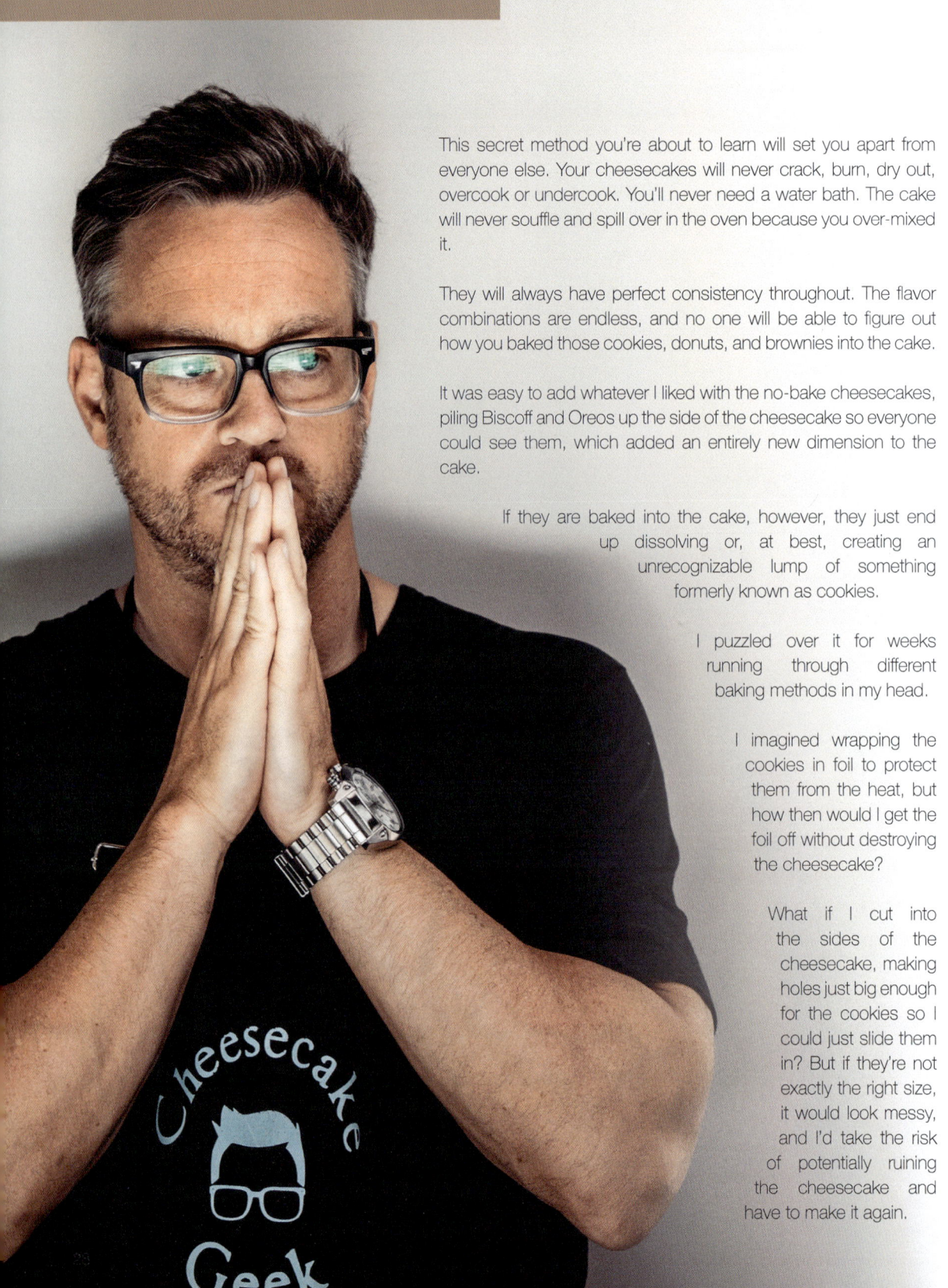

This secret method you're about to learn will set you apart from everyone else. Your cheesecakes will never crack, burn, dry out, overcook or undercook. You'll never need a water bath. The cake will never souffle and spill over in the oven because you over-mixed it.

They will always have perfect consistency throughout. The flavor combinations are endless, and no one will be able to figure out how you baked those cookies, donuts, and brownies into the cake.

It was easy to add whatever I liked with the no-bake cheesecakes, piling Biscoff and Oreos up the side of the cheesecake so everyone could see them, which added an entirely new dimension to the cake.

If they are baked into the cake, however, they just end up dissolving or, at best, creating an unrecognizable lump of something formerly known as cookies.

I puzzled over it for weeks running through different baking methods in my head.

I imagined wrapping the cookies in foil to protect them from the heat, but how then would I get the foil off without destroying the cheesecake?

What if I cut into the sides of the cheesecake, making holes just big enough for the cookies so I could just slide them in? But if they're not exactly the right size, it would look messy, and I'd take the risk of potentially ruining the cheesecake and have to make it again.

I was sure there had to be a way.

Then it struck me.

What if I bake the cheese mix separately, then once it's cooked, add it to the prepared biscuit base, with the cookies sitting in the tin waiting eagerly to have the cooked 'secret cheesecake mix' poured over them!

"It just might work"!?

I was excited to test it out. Will it work, or will the residual heat from the cheesecake just melt the cookies anyway?

IT WORKED!!!!!

I remember the joy. The cookies were in perfect condition! It also meant I could get the perfect consistency throughout the cake, from the edge to the center.

Because I didn't want the cheesecake mix to simply bake and set into the glass bowl, I had to stir the cheesecake mix as it baked.

As soon as it looked like it was setting around the edge of the bowl, I'd take it out of the oven and stir the mix together. A few lumps of cheesecake mix were setting quicker than others, but as I stirred them back in, the whole mix cooked evenly.

Then I thought "How am I going to know when it's ready?"

Usually, I use the "jiggle in the middle" test, but now the whole cheese mix is the same consistency, there is no jiggle in the middle?

'The jig was up!'

> I REMEMBER THE JOY, THE COOKIES WERE IN PERFECT CONDITION!

It took me a couple of attempts to get perfect, but I soon realized as long as you could form a 'peak' in the mix like you can with whipped cream and the mixture can hold itself without collapsing, you're good to go.

This meant that no matter what flavor the cheesecake was, I could just cook the cheesecake mix until it was at the consistency it needed to be. If it was lemon (because of the additional water content), then I'd cook it a little longer. If it's chocolate, then a little shorter, I can simply keep checking the mixture until it's ready.

So, this is **The Secret**. You're baking the cheesecake mix separately from the biscuit base. Once it's cooked, you pour the cooked cheesecake mix onto the prepared biscuit base.

Any other ingredients you want to use to decorate the sides of the cheesecake, biscuits, brownies, donuts, etc., won't melt and deform as they would if baked in a hot oven for an hour.

You simply arrange them in the cake tin wherever you like, then carefully pour the cheesecake mix into the tin, and ... Boom!!!

Perfectly baked cheesecake, no cracks, no water bath, no soggy bottoms.

I had created an entirely new way of baking cheesecakes. Please read through the method thoroughly before you start. Once you've baked your first few cheesecakes, you will realize the simplicity and potential of baking cheesecakes this way.

THE 'SECRET BAKING METHOD'

First, make the biscuit base you want to use, and pop it into the freezer while baking the 'secret cheesecake mix'.

1. Carefully pour the cheesecake mix into an oven-proof bowl, making sure not to get too much of the mix up the sides of the bowl. Any splashes of the cheesecake mix can brown quickly, so try to keep it from falling into the mix.

Place the bowl into the middle of the preheated oven.

2. After 20 minutes, take the bowl out of the oven. You will notice the edges starting to thicken. Carefully stir the mixture with your spatula, starting with the outer edge this bakes quicker than the middle, as will the bottom of the bowl. Scrape the bottom of the bowl and mix in lumps that start to form.

Note: Use your spatula to keep the sides of the bowl nice and clean.

Carefully place the bowl back in the oven for another 15 minutes.

Take it out again and give it another stir, breaking down the big lumps. Don't worry about any small lumps, as this is the cheese mix cooking.

Place it back in the oven again for a further 5 minutes. Take the cheesecake mix out and stir it again.

Note: at this point, the mix will start to thicken quickly and will look like it's starting to curdle, this is normal. Keep checking it every 5 minutes and give it a good stir.

Note: ALL ovens are different. Yours may cook the cheesecake mix slightly quicker, or it may take slightly longer. But it doesn't matter as long as you keep checking the consistency of the cheesecake mix.

3. Create a peak in the middle of the mix with your spatula to know when it's ready. The peak should be able to hold its own weight without collapsing. If it can't yet, pop it back in the oven for another 5 minutes.

Take it out of the oven and give it one last good stir. The cheesecake mix should be very thick, making a nice 'peak' easily and it will be ready to use.

Carefully pour the mix into a separate mixing bowl and give it a good stir, so there are no big lumps, and the mixture is even throughout.

Note: You can now add any additional flavors or colors you wish or create the marble effect at this stage.

4. Carefully pour it into your prepared cake tin, using a spatula to even the mixture out.

Be very careful with it, as it comes straight out of the oven, and it will be like red hot, delicious, sweet, creamy lava!

Pop it on a cake cooling rack until it's thoroughly cooled, which can take up to two hours. Place it in the fridge for at least 8 hours, preferably overnight, to chill and set.

Note: Because of the additional ingredients in some of the cheesecakes (donuts, etc.), you may occasionally have some of the mix leftover.

My advice is to grab a mug from the cupboard, put the excess cheesecake mix into it, let it cool, and then pop it in the fridge for a few hours.

Later that evening, grab a couple of cookies and a spoon!

Sit back, relax and enjoy your secret little mug of joy … (no one will ever know).

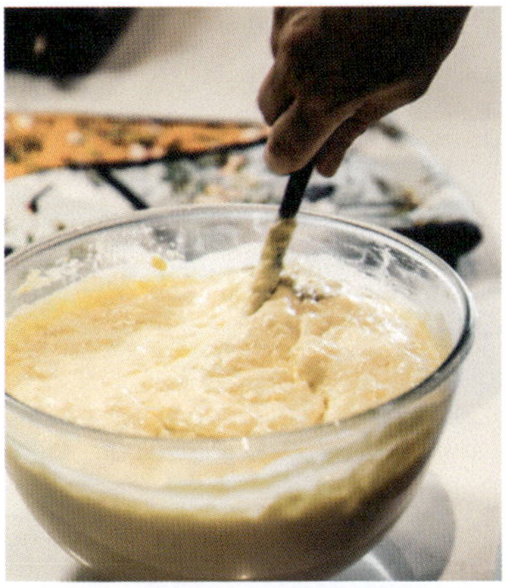
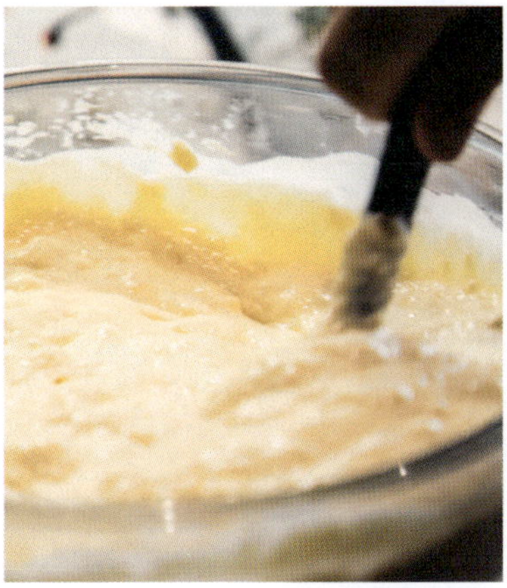
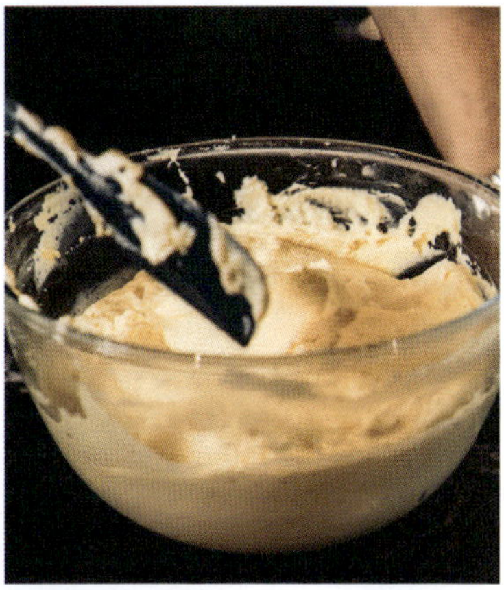
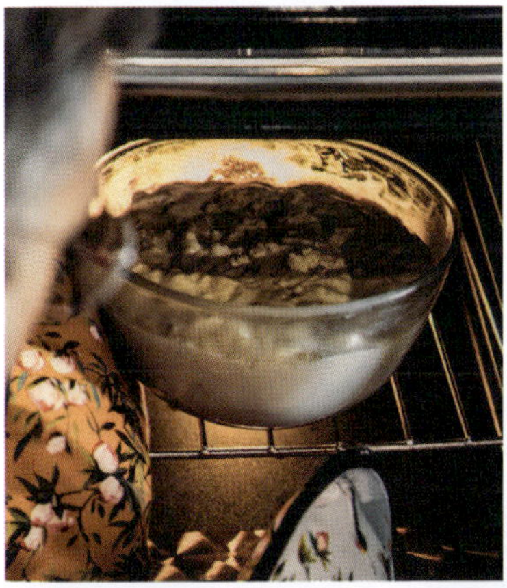
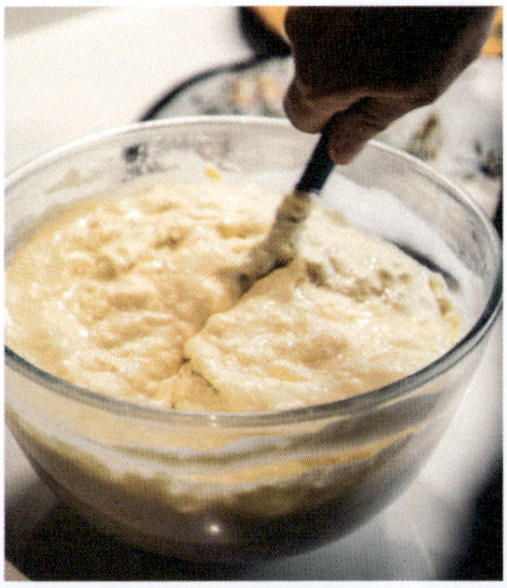
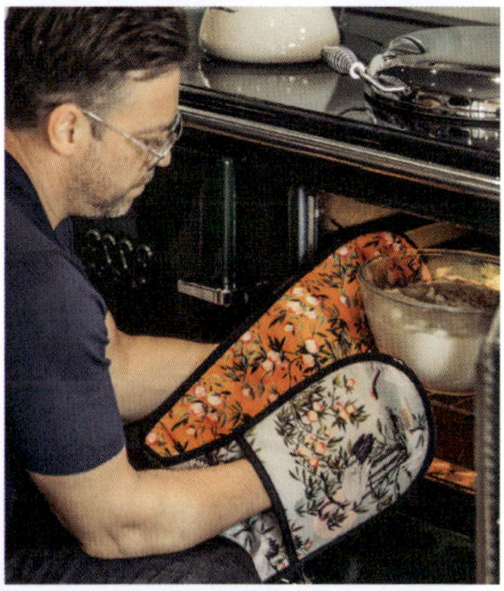
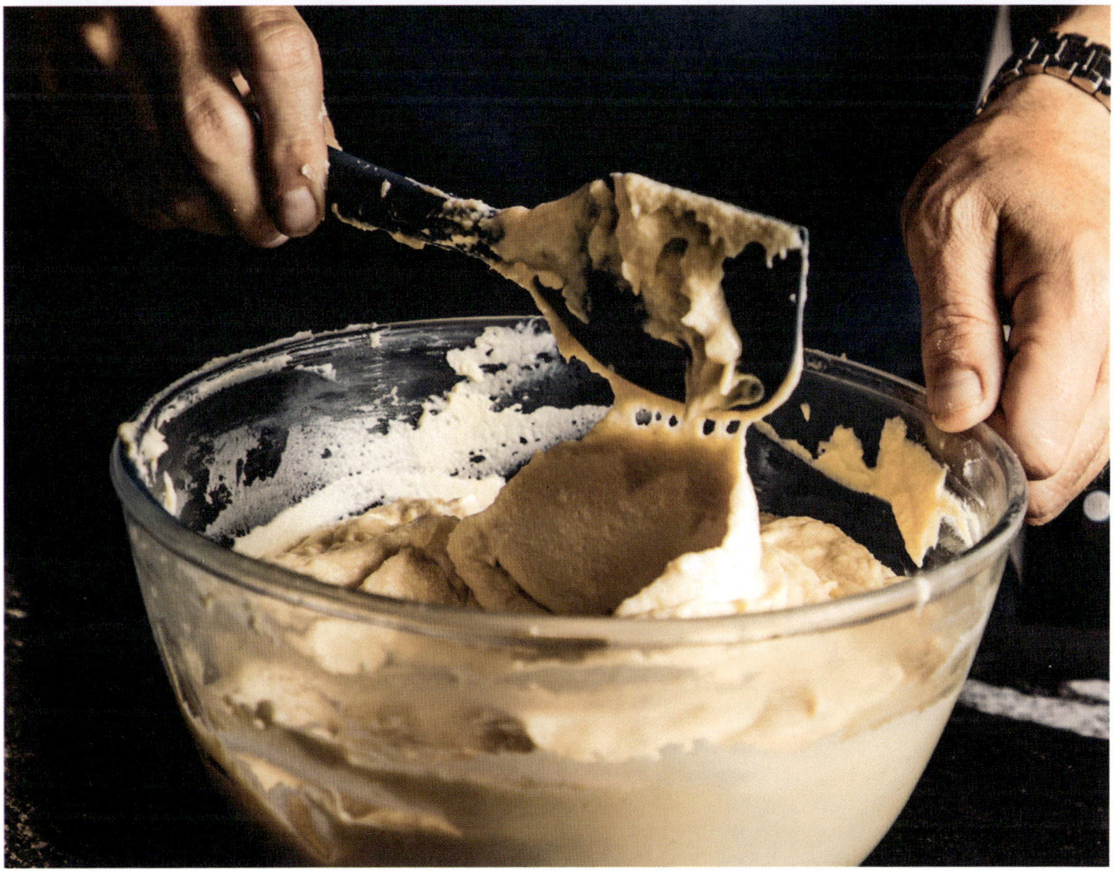

NETFLIX AND CHILLL'D

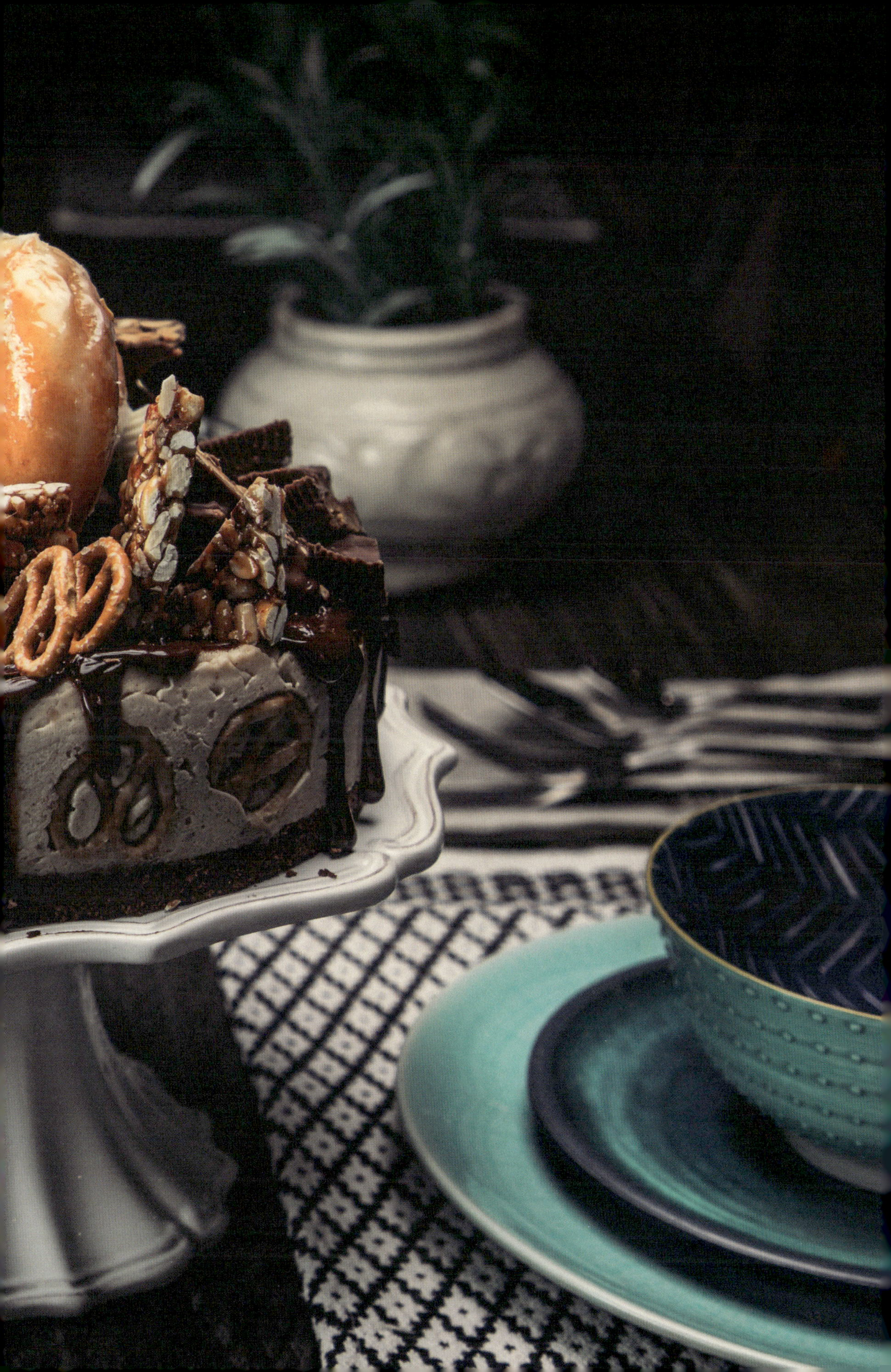

SPECIAL EFFECTS

The marble effect

This is a simple technique to do. It makes beautiful patterns on the sides and within the cake and will be unique every time. You can do this by adding different flavors and colors, using melted chocolate, caramel, food coloring, and flavor extracts.

For the chocolate marble

Ingredients
50g milk chocolate
50g dark chocolate

Microwave method:

Break the chocolate into a microwave-safe bowl. On a medium setting, melt the chocolate in 20-second bursts, reducing to 10 and 5 seconds as the chocolate melts, stirring every time, being careful not to burn it.

Hob/stovetop method:

Add the broken chocolate into a heat-proof bowl and place it onto a pan of barely simmering water, making sure the bottom of the bowl doesn't touch the simmering water. Gently stir until the chocolate is completely melted.

Once your 'cheesecake mix' is perfectly cooked and in a separate mixing bowl.
Pour the melted chocolate into one small section on the inside edge of the bowl, then slowly stir it in, using very small circles at first and slowly getting bigger until the chocolate is mixed with almost half of the cheesecake mix.

Get the prepared cake tin out of the freezer, and carefully pour the cheesecake mix into the tin from a height of about 12 inches. Depending on how you pour the mix into the tin will create different marble patterns.

The incredible marbling effect is created like this.

To make the top of the cake even and give it a nice glamorous finish, gently make circles with the flat edge of the spatula working your way into the middle.

You could add dark and white chocolate as well as caramel to the bowl of the cooked cheesecake mix, creating several different streaks of color and flavors, being careful not to mix them together in the bowl.

Use the exact same method for the coloring and flavor extracts. You could add several different colors and flavors into the bowl, creating a stunning rainbow of awesomeness. Your guests cannot fail to be impressed.

This is a straightforward, and easy way to make any cheesecake look beautiful.

SPECTACULAR LAYERS

Layering different flavors and colors also creates a beautiful effect with your cheesecakes. Any color and flavor combination you can think of will look amazing.

Separate the baked cheesecake mix into different bowls (two to four seems to be the ideal number for creating beautiful even layers).

Mix in the flavors and colors you wish into each different bowl of cheesecake mix.

Pour the first bowl into the prepared cake tin, leveling out the top with a spatula. Then carefully add each additional bowl of cheese mix on top of one another, leveling them out each time.

THE MARBLE EFFECT

THE ZEBRA STRIPE

Separate the cheesecake mix evenly into two bowls.

Add some food coloring or a flavor (e.g. chocolate or caramel) into each half and mix until it's thoroughly combined.

Pour approximately a quarter of one of the cheesecake mixes into the center of the biscuit base.

Then, carefully pour a quarter of the other mix directly onto the middle of the first mix.

Keep alternating, pouring the two mixes on top of each other until there is none left.

Even out the surface with your spatula.

By layering the two mixes this way, you create the elegant zebra stripe effect, which can be used for any of the other cheesecakes, creating fabulous colorful stripes throughout the cake.

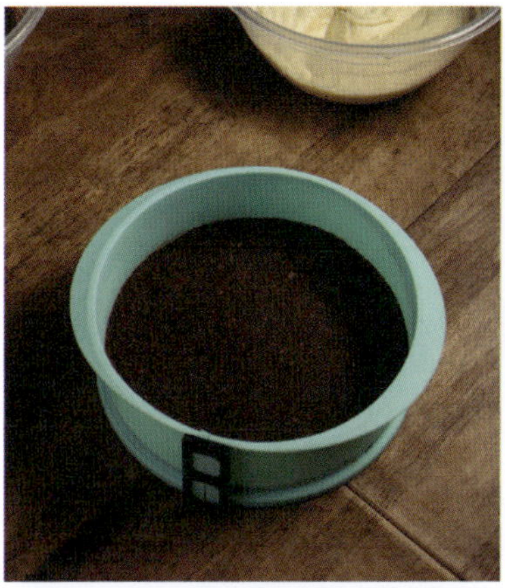
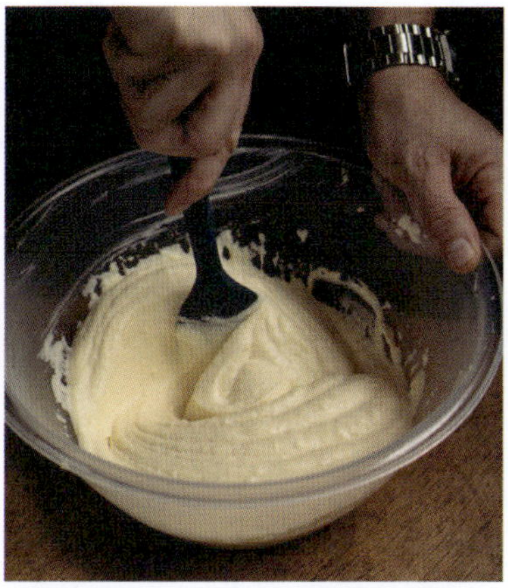
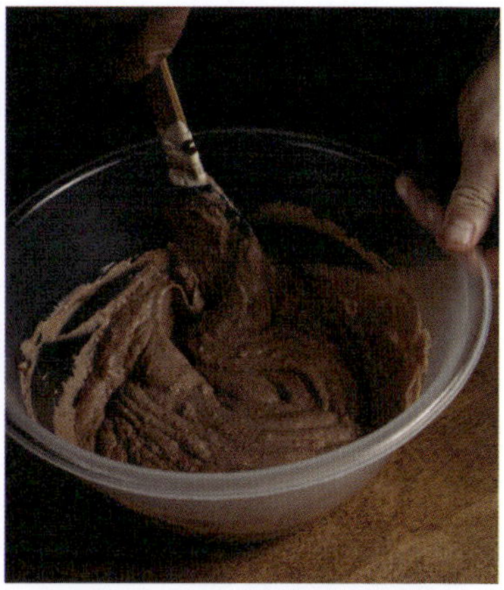
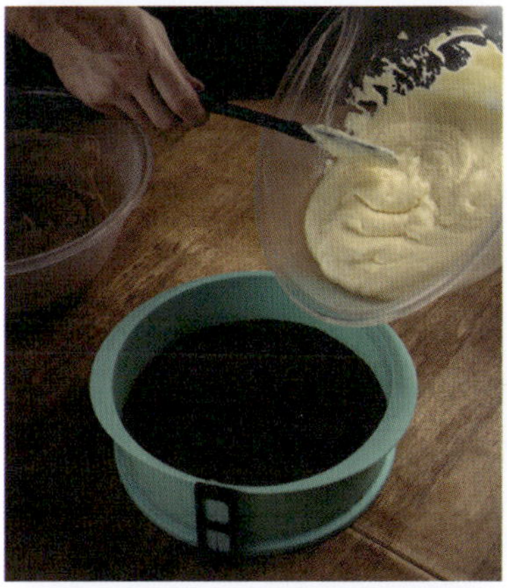
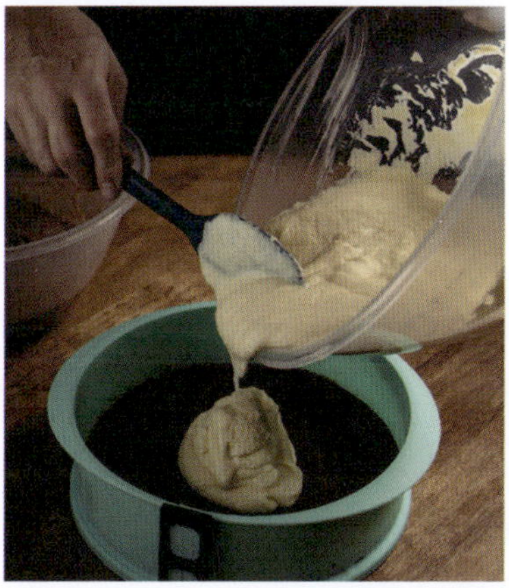
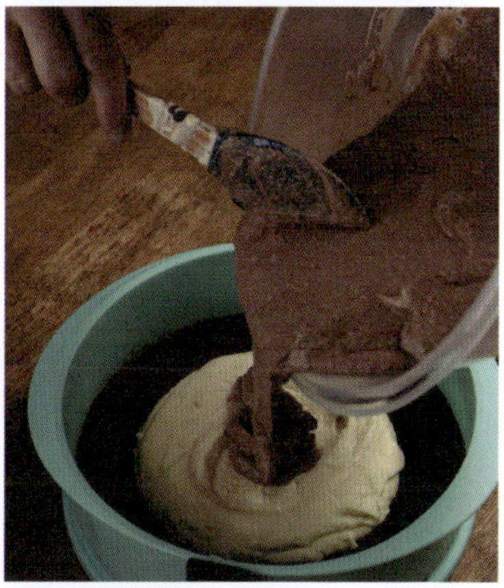
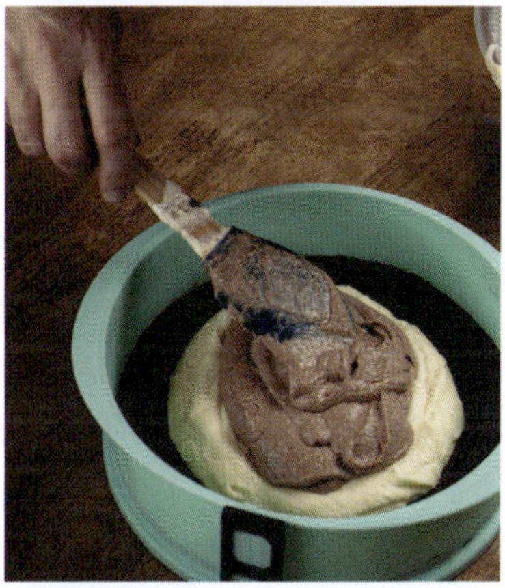
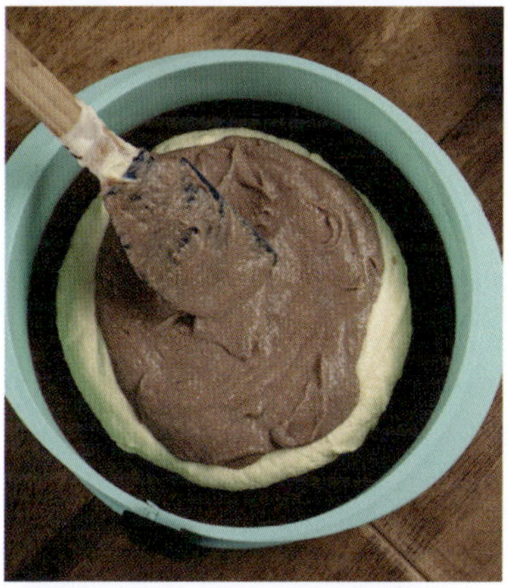
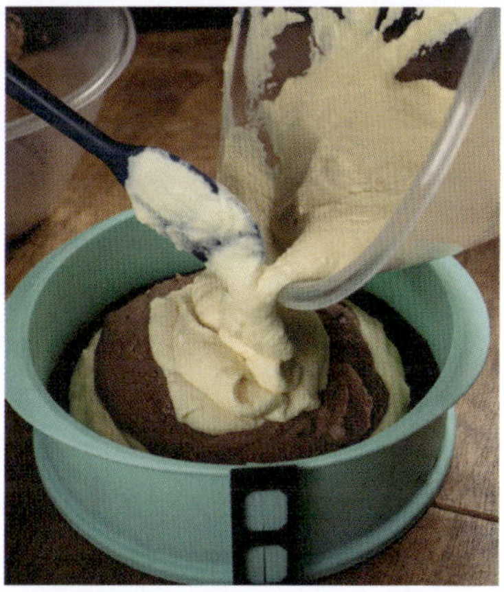
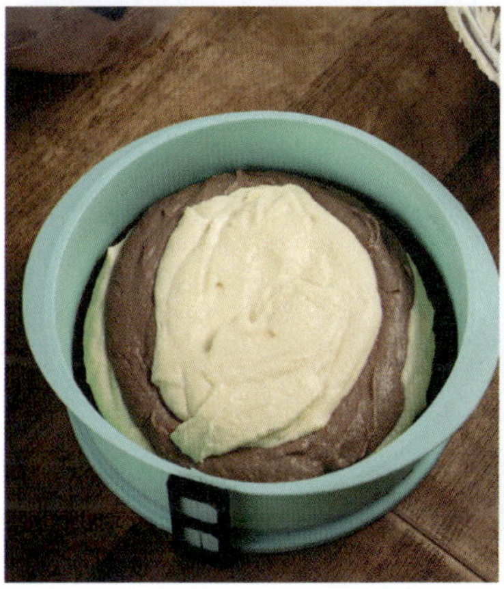
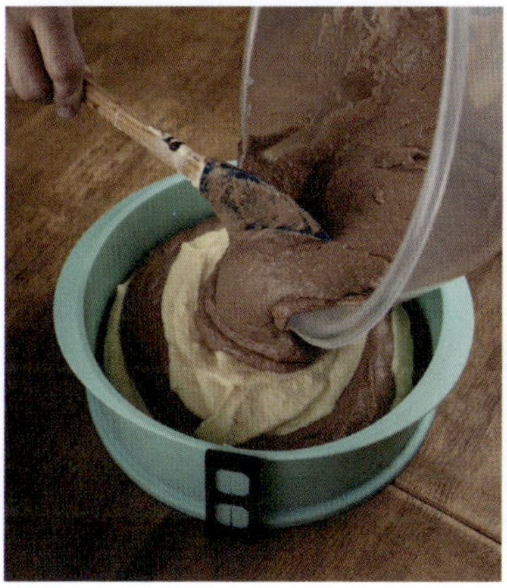
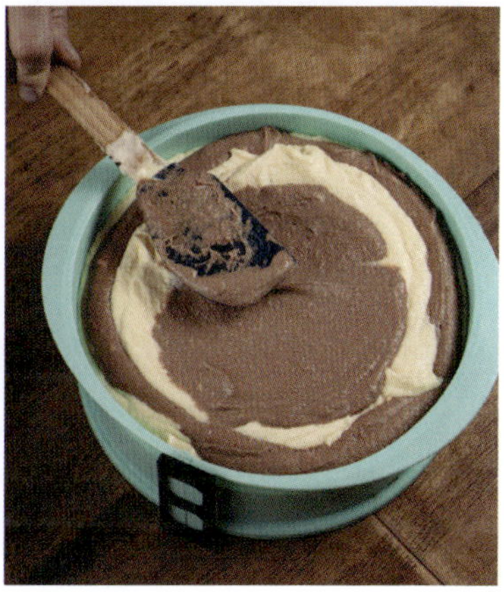

ADDING DONUTS/ COOKIES/ BROWNIES ETC

Place the cookies/brownies/donuts into the tin.

You want them all to be exposed for your amazed guests to see, so push them to the inner wall touching the sides of the cake tin.

Gently pour all the mix into the tin. You might need to use a spatula to make sure the mix gets around all the grooves of the additional goodies.

For the 'Peek-a-boo' effect, stack a few cookies on one another, just so they come halfway up the tin, and pour the mix in as usual.

Before you put the cheesecake into the fridge to chill and firm up

If you're using a steel springform tin, and once the cake has cooled down enough for you to pick up, gently tip the tin at a slight angle towards you, so gravity pulls the cheesecake away from the top of the tin. Turn the tin slowly in a circle keeping it tipped slightly (like you're turning a car's steering wheel).

You will see the cake pull away from the sides of the tin.

This ensures the cake comes away cleanly when you take it out of the tin and prevents any of it from sticking as it cools.

You'll be left with perfectly smooth sides to the cake.

Leave it in the fridge overnight to chill.

If you have a silicone cake tin, it won't stick, so you don't need to do this step.

All springform cake tins will naturally leave a slight groove down one side of the cake because of the split in the tin, so pile up the brownies, biscuits right next to the groove to hide it or make your first chocolate drip down the groove.

38

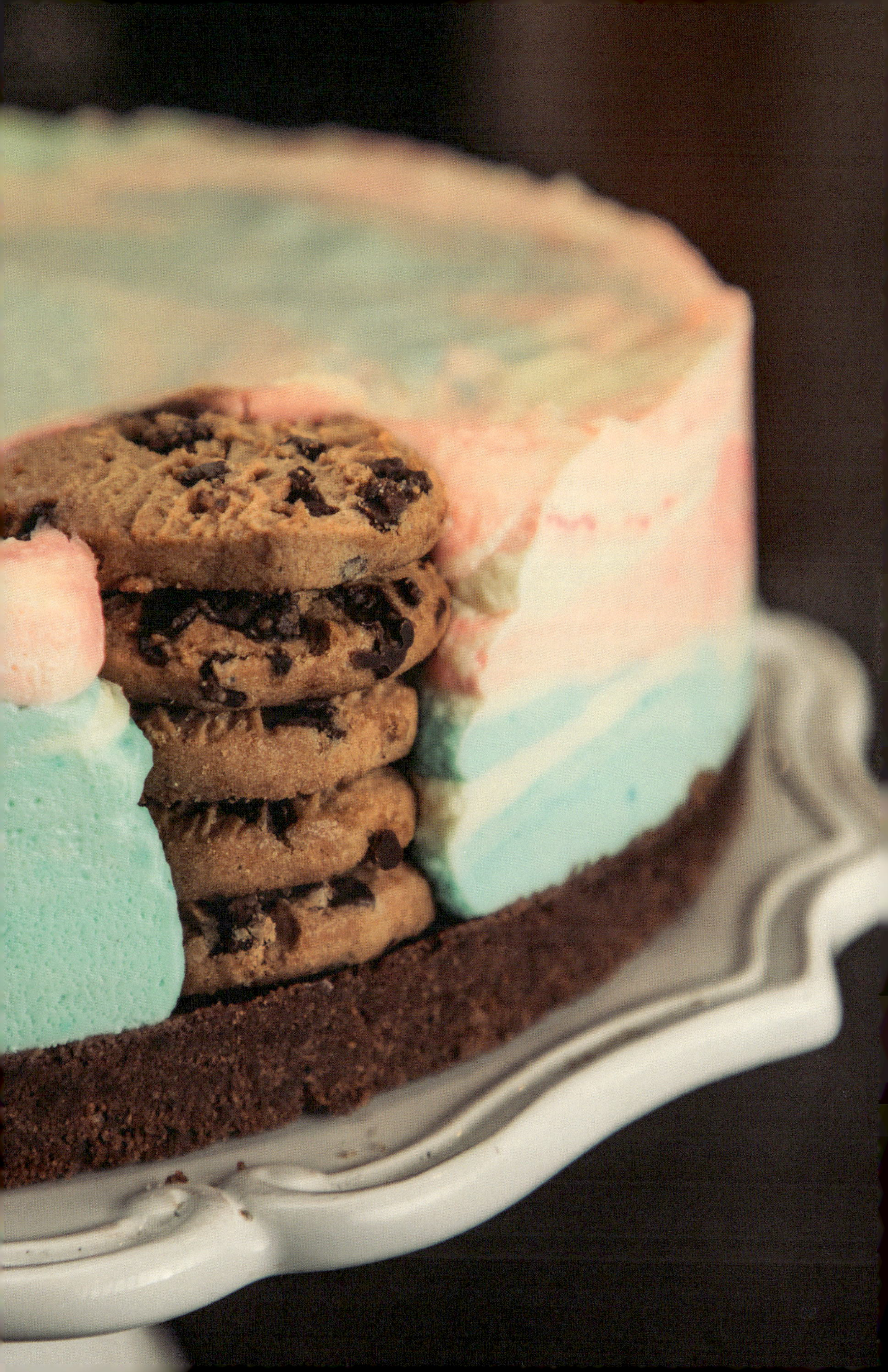

MINI CHOCOLATE PIPING BAG

This little bag of melted joy will come in handy when you need to stick the cheesecake to the cake board, as well as for decorating the donuts.

Break 20g of milk or white chocolate into a small sandwich bag, then melt it slowly in the microwave, on low heat, and at 20-second intervals, make sure there are no lumps that could block the piping hole.

Once it's all melted and you can't feel any lumps, tie the end of the bag in a knot (if you can) so no chocolate leaks out, and cut a tiny piece from the corner of the bag so it's ready to use as a mini piping bag.

REMOVING THE CHEESECAKE FROM THE TIN

Steel springform tin

Carefully release the sides of the springform tin and lift it off.

Then place a piece of cling film/Saran wrap onto the top of the cake and then a light chopping board. Thin plastic ones are best as we don't want to crush the cake.

Carefully flip the cake upside down and remove the base of the cake tin.

Pipe a circle of chocolate in the middle of the cake board with the chocolate piping bag. Place the board on the upside-down cheesecake (chocolate facing down).

Flip the cake back around and place it on a cake stand.

Remove the chopping board and the cling film.

Place the cheesecake into the freezer while you make the ganache.

This will ensure the ganache drips set quickly on the cold cake as they drip down the edges.

If you're using a silicone cake tin

Pull the plastic holding pin out.
Carefully peel back the silicone sides, pulling away with both ends.

Using a cake lifter or pizza peel, slide it under the cake and lift it off the glass base. Lower the cheesecake onto the cake board, pulling the cake lifter away quickly in one smooth motion.

Place the cheesecake into the freezer while you make the ganache.

The ganache drips set quickly as they run down the edge of the cold cake.

The chocolate drip will make your guests want to dive headfirst into the cake. There's nothing more decadent than melting chocolate running down the side of a cake.

Ganache is simply a mixture of chocolate and cream. It can be used as a glaze, sauce, filling, frosting, or to make truffles, and a filling and coating in cakes. A larger proportion of chocolate to cream creates a "firm" ganache that has the consistency of thick paste at room temperature, which hardens upon refrigeration.

This type of ganache is often formed into balls and rolled in cocoa powder to create simple truffles, which can be used for decorating. The texture of the ganache will depend on the ratio of cream to chocolate. The larger proportion of cream creates a "loose" or "soft" ganache that is relatively liquid at room temperature, perfect for filling molded chocolates and for creating the amazing drip we're using for the cheesecakes.

In its most basic state, ganache is made by simmering cream, pouring the hot cream over the chopped chocolate, and then whisking the mixture until the chocolate is completely melted and incorporated. The easier method is to melt the chocolate and the cream together in slow bursts in a microwave.

Note: Different chocolate brands behave differently, and depending on the temperature and humidity of where you live, it will affect the ganache. So it's good to do a test drip on the side of a glass before you start. For the most consistent results, once you find the chocolate to cream ratio you like, stick to those brands.

Milk chocolate

50g dark/semi-sweet chocolate
50g milk chocolate
100 ml heavy/double cream

Microwave method

Break the chocolate into pieces and pop into a microwavable jug.

Add 100ml heavy/double cream.

Microwave on medium heat, stirring every 20 seconds until all the chocolate has melted and it drips off the spoon.

Hot cream method

Break the chocolate into small pieces into a measuring jug.

Heat the cream on the stovetop and pour over the chocolate.

Leave it for 30 seconds and then gently stir until all the chocolate has melted and there are no more lumps.

White chocolate

100g white chocolate
40 ml heavy/double cream

Use the same methods as above, but note the white chocolate will melt much quicker than milk and dark chocolate.

If you find the ganache is too thin, it will thicken as it cools, but if you find it's still a little runny, chop or grate some more chocolate into the ganache, and stir it until it's completely dissolved.

Creating an elegant drip

With half a spoonful of the ganache start at one edge of the cake. If the groove from the tin is visible, run the first drip down the groove, it will then be hidden from everyone.

Allow the ganache to slowly fall off the spoon, dripping down the edge of the cold cake. If the ganache runs down the cake quickly onto the cake board, it's too thin or too hot.

Continue this around the whole cake. Drip the ganache at uneven intervals rather than uniformly to make it look natural. Make some shorter and some longer, with one or two of them hitting the cake board.

You want it to look as if you've just poured a giant bowl of chocolate onto the cheesecake, and it's running over the edges naturally.

Adding food coloring to white chocolate ganache

While the ganache is warm, add a few drops of concentrated coloring or gel and stir it well. Be careful not to add too much liquid as this will change the consistency of the ganache, and it could become too runny.

Blue and pink work well on a vanilla or white chocolate cake, but use your favorite colors to add contrast to the cake.

THE SALTED CARAMEL DIP

45

DECORATING A SPECTACULAR CHEESECAKE

Your artistic talent comes to the fore here. You can add almost anything to your cake, just as long as it's not too heavy! I've had full bottles of Moet on them, so they can take quite a bit of weight.

As you decorate it, be mindful of balance. The size, texture, and color are the main factors. Generally, place the tallest items in the middle and the smaller ones at the edges. Donuts are usually the centerpiece, and slice your favorite chocolates on an angle revealing their contents, which adds detail to the cake. Lean the chocolate bars on one another at different angles.

The cake wants to look fully loaded but not messy. Over time you will find your individual style of decorating. Use fruit, as these naturally beautiful and delicious decorations only need placing neatly onto the cake, instantly adding color and beautiful shapes.

Strawberries cut in half with the green stem on add a beautiful freshness to the cake. These could be mixed with carefully chosen chocolates to make a sophisticated-looking cheesecake.

Before you start to decorate the cake, place the cheesecake into the freezer while you prepare the toppings, this will help the ganache drips set quicker, making them look more natural.

Get all your toppings ready, donuts decorated, fruit washed, and chocolates unwrapped and sliced. You'll need to melt the chocolate piping bag you used to stick the cake to the board to decorate the donuts, and the ganache will need to be warmed and ready to start dripping.

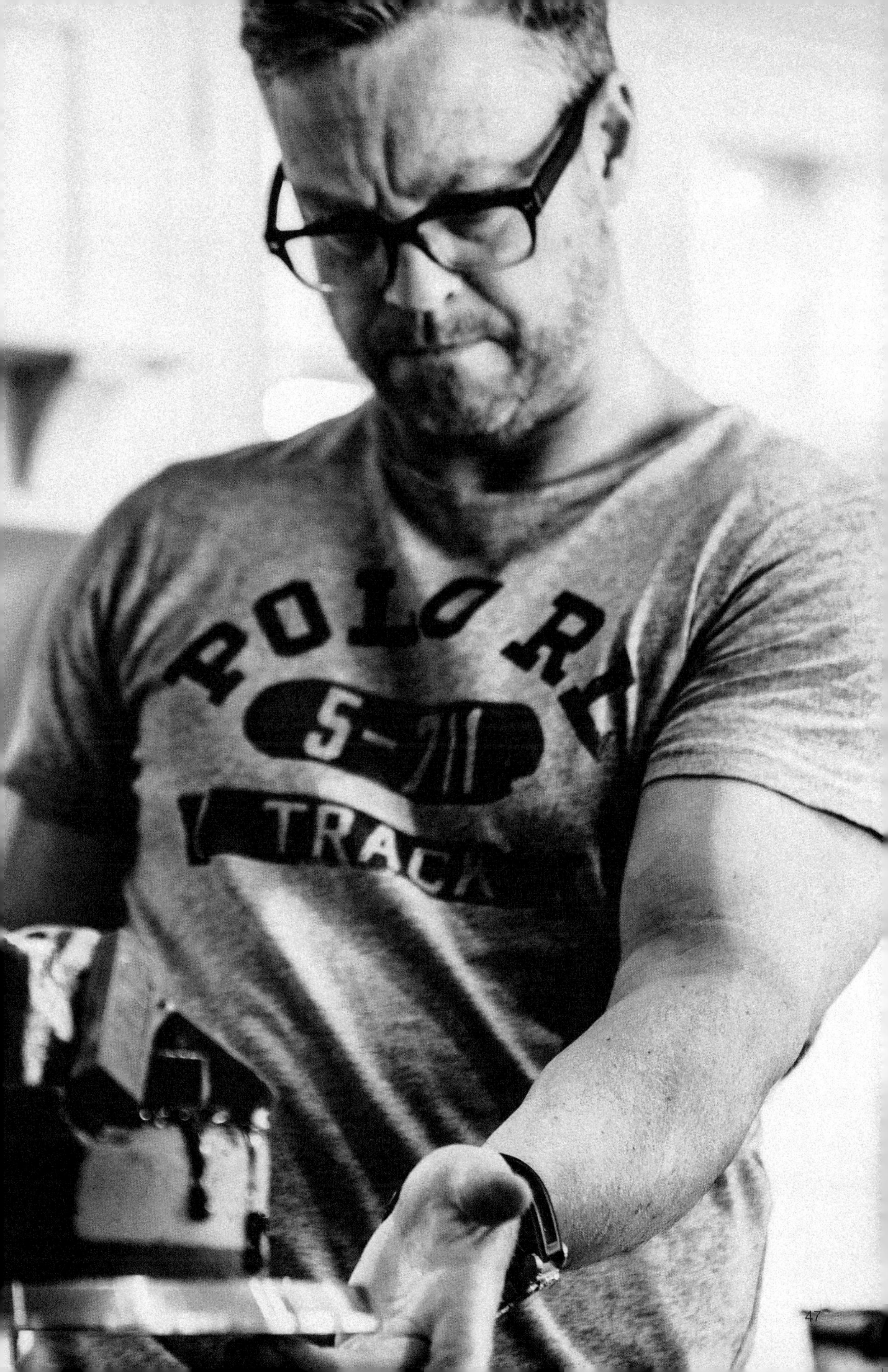

48

CHOCOLATE FUDGE BROWNIE

CUSTOMIZING THE DONUTS

Donuts come in different flavors and colors, but you can always customize them to make them your own. Dipping them into the ganache and then sprinkling them with nuts, chocolate shavings, M & M's, or edible flowers, and piping chocolate stripes onto them.

Personalize each one for each cake. You can also personalize the mini donuts, as these make beautifully delicious, bite-size decorations for your cheesecake.

Put the donuts into the freezer for at least 20 minutes. This ensures the ganache sets quickly.

Make the ganache as instructed. You can add food coloring to white chocolate ganache to customize it even further.

Using a fork, stab the lucky donut and dip it into the ganache, pushing the donut down into it, so the ganache comes halfway up the sides of the donut.
Lift it back out, and allow the excess to drip off back into the jug.

Place the freshly 'ganached' donut onto a plate or chopping board (ganache side up) and decorate it however you like. Be creative, use your imagination, and they will look amazing.

Place them into the fridge to set.

Piping chocolate stripes

Use the chocolate piping bag you used to stick the cheesecake to the board. These are so simple to do and look incredibly elegant. You can use milk, dark or white chocolate, and even add a tiny drop of food coloring to make any color you choose.

Carefully cut the corner off the sandwich bag with a pair of scissors. I find a smaller hole makes a more elegant stripe.

Take the donuts out of the fridge. By now, the ganache should be completely set. Gently squeeze the piping bag to make sure the chocolate comes out smoothly.

Working from one side of the donut to the other, draw the stripes onto it, making sure you run over each side of the donut by an inch or so.

You could have one-half stripes and the other half decorated in chocolate or edible flowers like I've done here. I even flicked edible gold liquid onto them using a toothpick.

Draw checks or even circles onto the donuts, and if you're feeling confident, you could write someone's name onto them or a nice message.

PERSONALIZED RECIPES

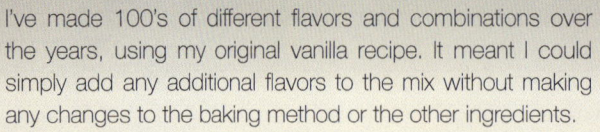

I've made 100's of different flavors and combinations over the years, using my original vanilla recipe. It meant I could simply add any additional flavors to the mix without making any changes to the baking method or the other ingredients.

Now you can create your own perfect, totally original, delicious cheesecakes for your family and friends. Tailor-make each cheesecake for every occasion, a completely personalized and unique cheesecake every time.

RECIPES

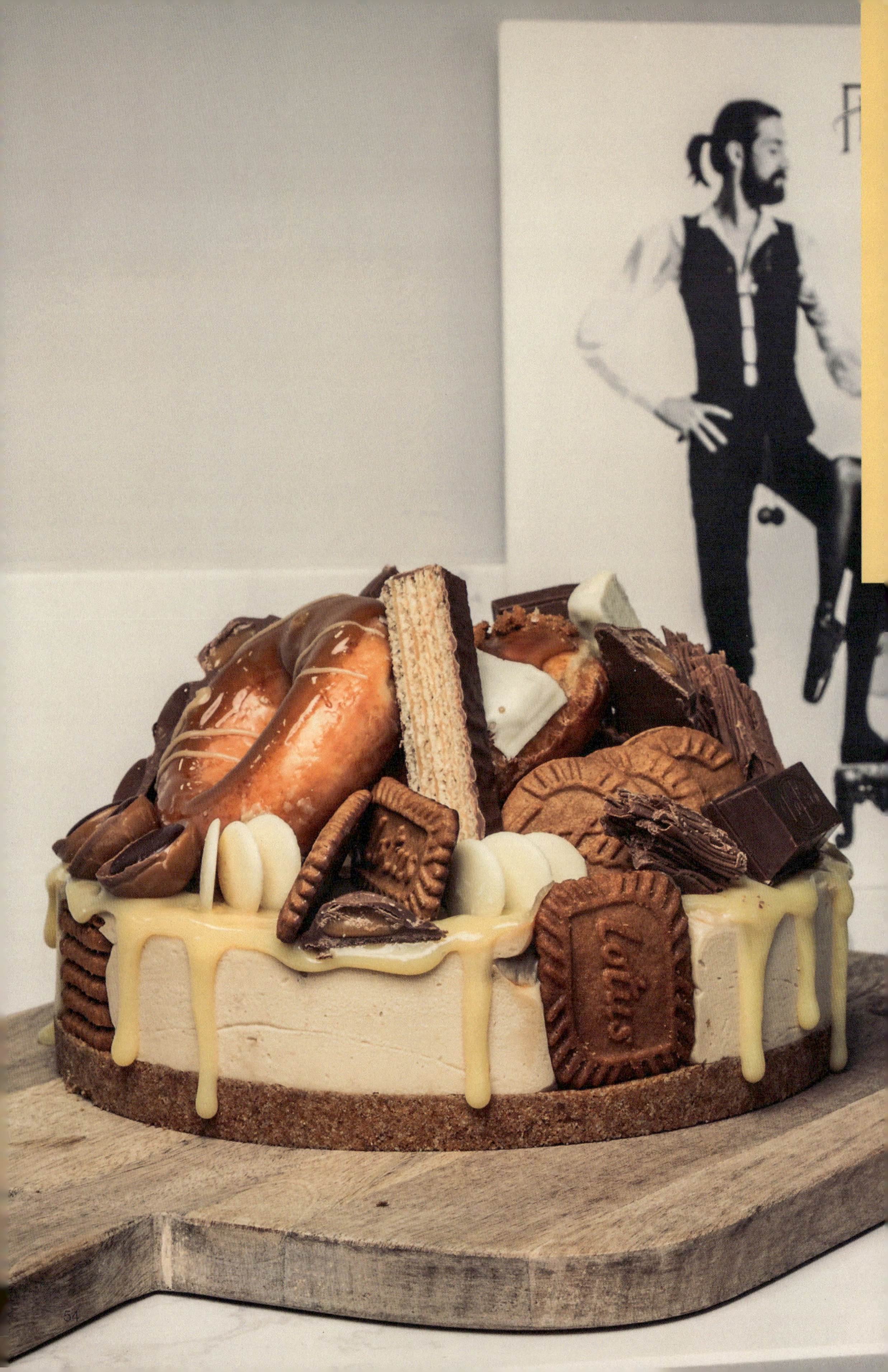
Lotus

BISCOFF

Ingredients

200g Biscoff spread (or crushed biscuits if you can't get the spread)
100g Biscoff biscuits, broken up

When I first made a Biscoff cheesecake, I knew it would be good, but I had no idea just how delicious it would be. Biscoff are probably my favorite biscuits. If you've never tried them before, you don't know what you're missing.

Biscoff are caramelized shortcrust biscuits with warm spices which make a deep sweet caramel flavor. In Europe, many cafés, and restaurants will serve you a single Biscoff biscuit with your coffee as a delicious mini dessert.

The Biscoff cheesecake is probably my favorite cheesecake of all (along with salted caramel, cherry Bakewell and Key Lime. Oh, and the lemon and the Reeses, and the Krispy Kreme).

Biscoff are my favorite biscuits, with an irresistible melt-in-the-mouth consistency and sweet caramel that go perfectly together. It is a better combination than milk chocolate, I think. The recipe could easily be converted by changing the white to milk chocolate.

That's the beauty of cheesecakes and these recipes. You do what you want.

Method

Mix the Biscoff/Speculoos biscuits or spread into the baked cheesecake mix.

Add the broken Biscoff biscuits into the baked cheesecake mix and fold them into the creamy cheesecake goodness.

Stack some Biscoff around the edges of the tin on top of each other and on their side with the logo facing out so your cheesecake can proudly exclaim to everyone what flavor it is.

Pour into the prepared cake tin.

Cool and chill.

YOUR NOTES

INSPIRATION

THE WHITE CHOCOLATE BISCOFF IS FANTASTIC AND ONE OF THE MOST POPULAR AT CHEESECAKE GEEK. SIMPLY MIX 150G OF GOOD QUALITY MELTED WHITE CHOCOLATE AND MIX IT INTO THE BAKED CHEESECAKE MIX

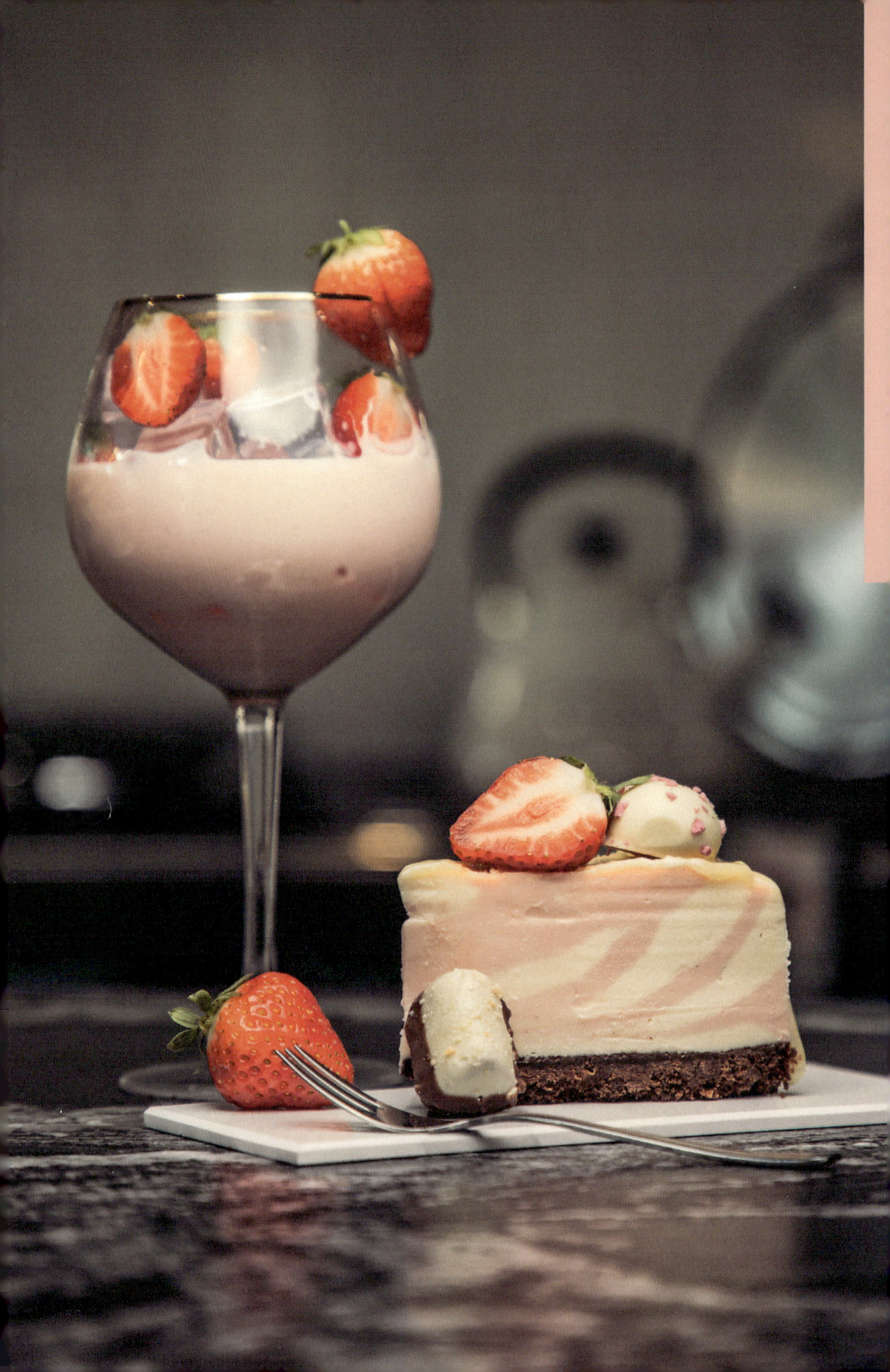

STRAWBERRIES AND CREAM BAILEYS

Ingredients

200g good quality white chocolate
200 ml strawberries and cream Baileys
8 drops pink food coloring

This is the perfect summer cheesecake. I've made dozens of Bailey's cheesecakes before, and they're delicious, but as soon as the strawberries and cream version came out, I knew it would make an incredible cheesecake.

The 'zebra stripe' effect will look elegant and beautiful when you slice a piece for one of your guests at your summer garden party.

Method

Melt the white chocolate and mix it into the cheese mix.

Add in the Baileys and mix again until all the liquid is combined.

'Bake the Secret way'.

Separate the cheesecake mix evenly into two bowls.

Add the pink food coloring into one half and mix until combined. It should be a lovely baby pink color.

Carefully pour approximately a quarter of the white mix onto the center of the biscuit base.

Then pour a quarter of the pink mix directly onto the middle of the white mix.

Keep alternating, pouring the two mixes until there is none left.

By layering the two mixes this way, you create the elegant zebra stripe effect, which can be used for any of the other cheesecakes, creating attractive, colorful stripes throughout the cake.

YOUR NOTES

INSPIRATION

REPLACE THE STRAWBERRIES AND CREAM WITH ANY OF THE OTHER FLAVORS OF BAILEYS AND MAKE YOUR OWN UNIQUE CREATIONS

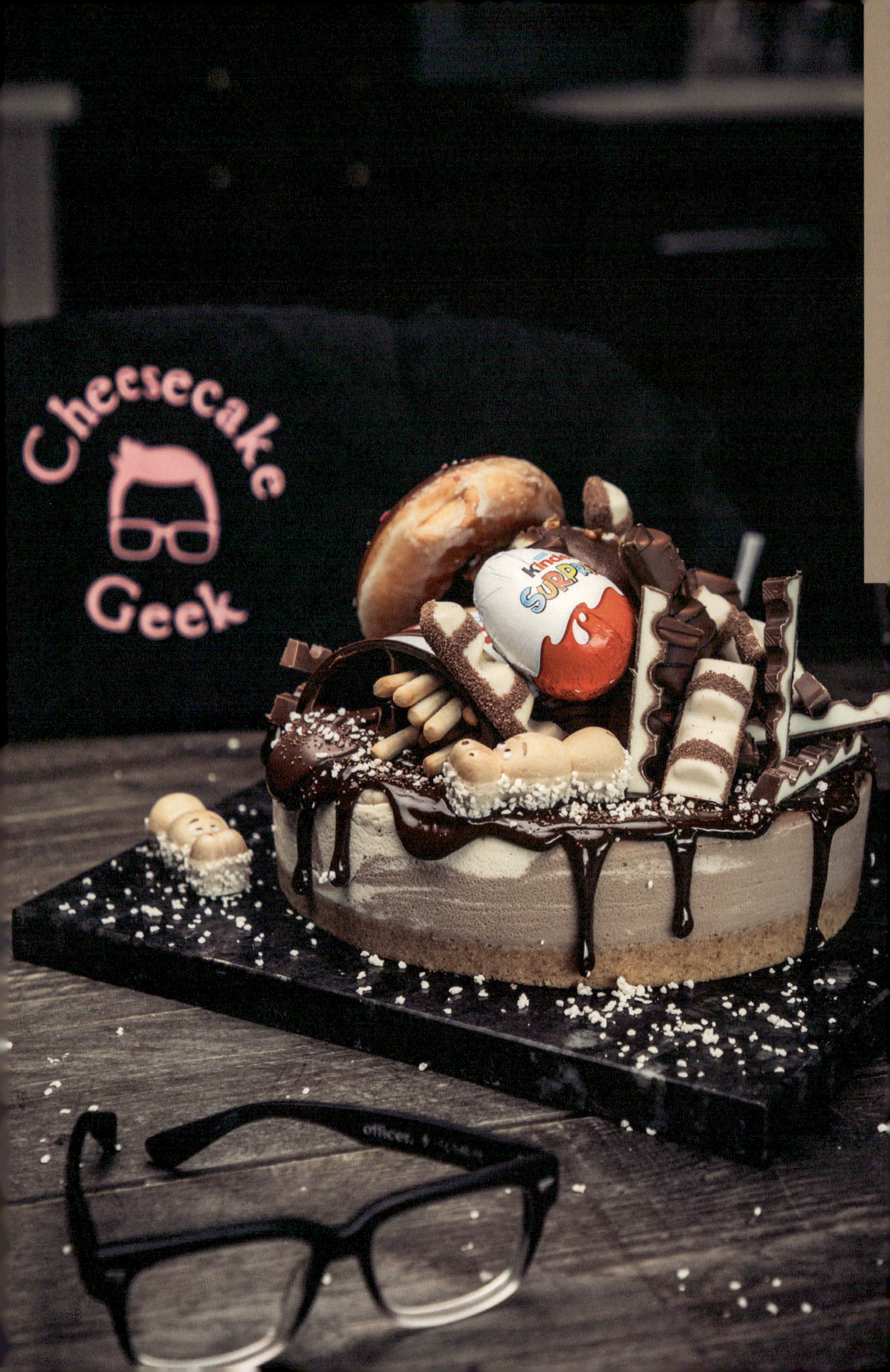
Cheesecake
Geek

KINDER MADNESS

Ingredients

50g good quality dark chocolate
100g Nutella

The Kinder cheesecake is probably the most popular cheesecake I've made, an absolute showstopper. The vanilla and Nutella cheesecake is beautifully marbled and topped with a Nutella dip, Buenos, Kinder chocolates, and a Krispy Kreme donut.

A chocolate biscuit base works best with this cheesecake. I made it once for a customer with an additional Biscoff swirl, as well as the Nutella. What can I say? Biscoff just improves life.

Method

Melt the chocolate.

Mix the chocolate with the Nutella until it's thoroughly combined.

Using the marbling method, mix the chocolate Nutella into approximately half of the baked cheesecake mixture.

Gently pour the Nutella/vanilla mix from a height of about 12 inches onto the biscuit base, creating the marble effect.

Cool and chill as usual.

YOUR NOTES

INSPIRATION

ADD BROKEN KINDER BUENOS INTO THE MIX JUST BEFORE YOU POUR IT INTO THE CAKE TIN. WHAT ABOUT ADDING A BISCOFF SWIRL? HMMM?

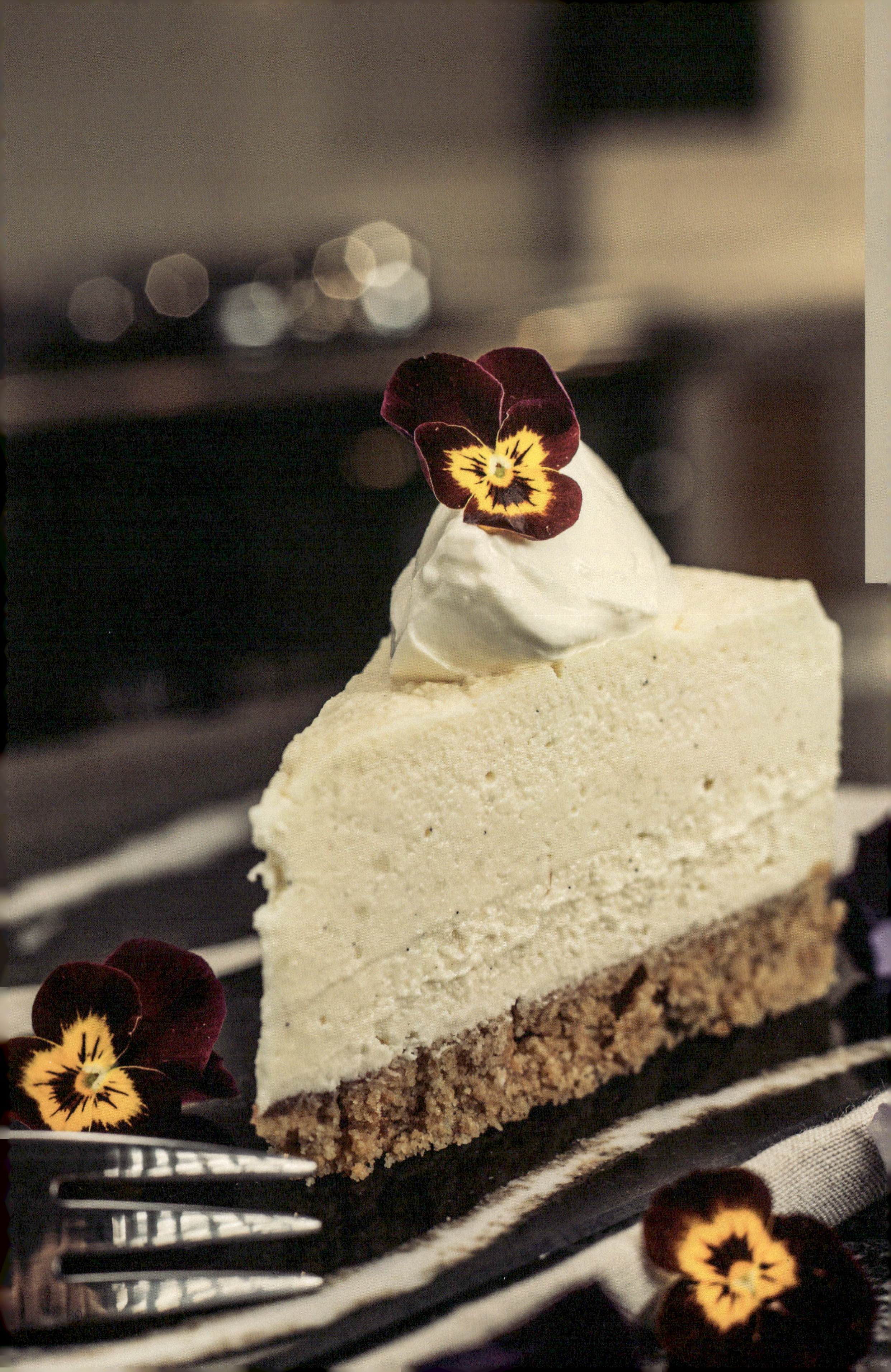

NEW YORK-STYLE

Ingredients

½ teaspoon of vanilla extract
The zest of a whole lemon and
1.5 teaspoon lemon juice
2 egg yolks

The classic that started it all, dating back to the 1920s. A man named Arnold Ruben has been credited with inventing the most popular cheesecake on earth. Every good restaurant has its own version, differing slightly from the next but sticking to the main ingredients.

It is delicious on its own but on another level with some fruit compote.

With the addition of the extra egg yolks, the New York cheesecake is known to be slightly richer and more indulgent than the standard vanilla cheesecakes. A hint of lemon adds a nice zing and sourness without overpowering the flavor and turning it into a lemon cheesecake.

It can be topped with anything, milk, dark and white chocolate, or any fruit and any flavor of donut.

As the base cheesecake mix is almost New York-style, all you need to do is add in a few extra ingredients to the base mix before you bake it.

Method

Separate the two egg yolks and mix them in until they have disappeared completely.

Zest the lemon into the bowl.

Add the juice and mix well.

Pour into the prepared cake tin.

Graham/Digestive biscuit base is the traditional choice, but feel free to use any base you like.

YOUR NOTES

INSPIRATION

USE THE MARBLING TECHNIQUE TO MIX IN A SALTED CARAMEL OR CHOCOLATE SWIRL AND MAYBE ADD SOME BROWNIES

62

THE SALTED CARAMEL DIP

Ingredients

For the cheesecake:
250 g of Dulce de leche caramel
1-1.5 teaspoon salt For the dip:
200 g Dulce de leche caramel (or your favorite caramel)
20g double/heavy cream
½ teaspoon salt (or to taste)

The perfect sharing cheesecake is the salted caramel dip cake, a real party piece. A perfectly balanced sweet and salty cheesecake with a luxurious salted caramel dip in the middle. The idea is everyone can pick the toppings from it and dip them into the salted caramel deliciousness. Absolutely no double-dipping, please! (Offenders ideally should be warned then instantly barred).

Caramel from a tin or jar works perfectly well, but I've included a fantastic recipe for those who are feeling adventurous. Your taste buds will thank you.

Method

Mix 1 tsp of salt into 300g of Dulche de leche caramel. Mix the caramel evenly into the cheese mix.

'Bake using the secret method'.

Pour into a prepared cake tin.

For the dip:

Mix the Dulce de leche, salt, and cream together.
Once you're ready to decorate, use the empty caramel tin, a cup, or mug to mark a nice, neat circle in the middle of the cake. Grab a spoon and carefully start scooping out a 2" deep crater in the middle of the cheesecake, then fill it with the salted caramel.

You will want to top this with things your guests can easily pick off, pretzels, brownies, Reese's cups sliced in half, and any wafer biscuits are perfect. Chop your favorite chocolates into bite-size pieces for this one.

YOUR NOTES

INSPIRATION

CHANGE THE DIP TO ANYTHING YOU LIKE - FOR EXAMPLE, MIX 50ML DOUBLE/HEAVY CREAM WITH 175G OF NUTELLA

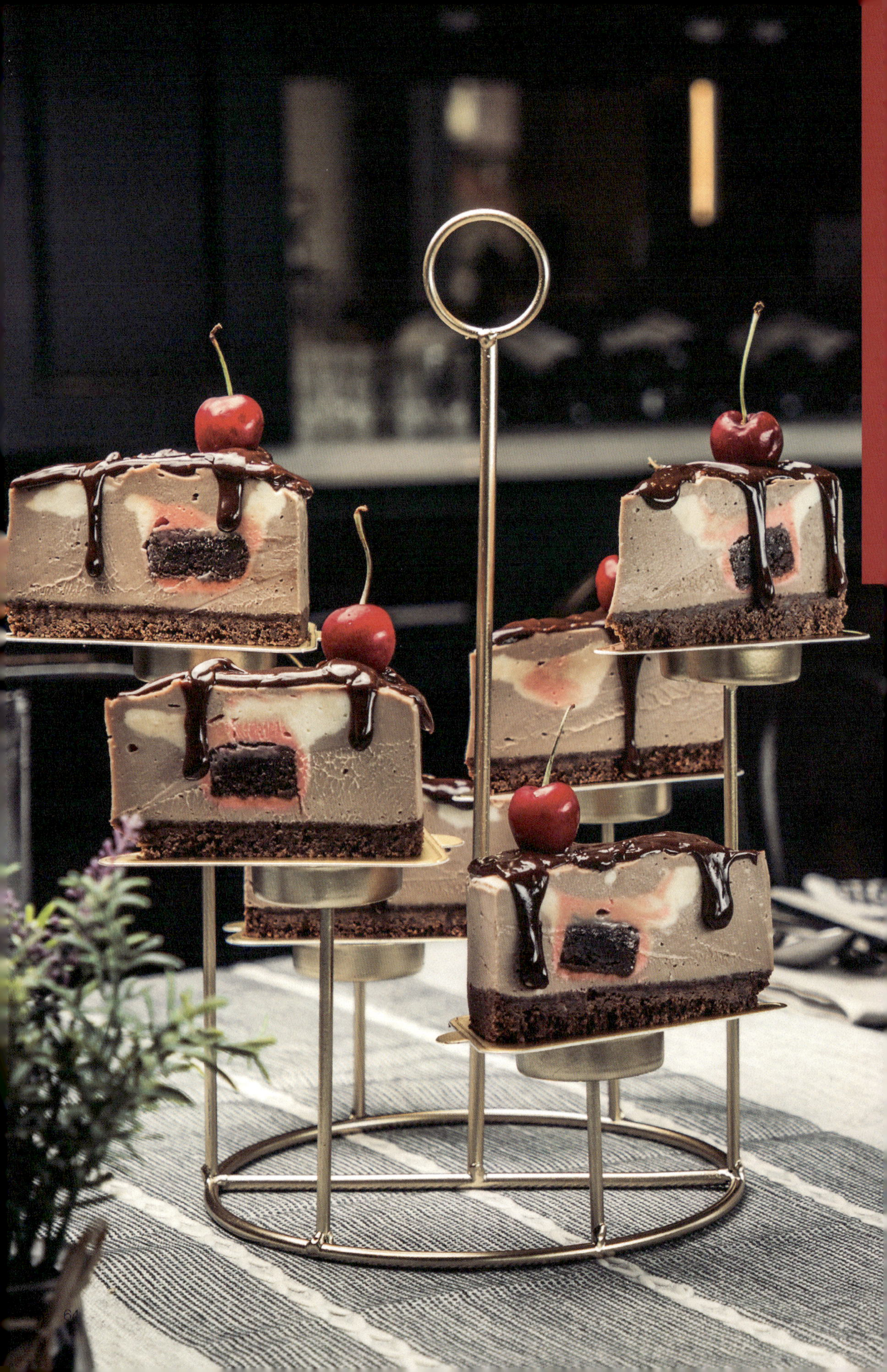

CHERRY NUTELLA BROWNIE

Ingredients

100 g good quality dark chocolate
150g Nutella
200g brownies cut into 1-inch pieces
4 drops black cherry flavoring
5 drops cherry food coloring

YOUR NOTES

This cheesecake looks incredible when you slice it. You see the deliciously moist chocolate brownie floating in a sea of Nutella surrounded by gorgeous pink and white cherry and vanilla cheesecake. It's almost too good to eat (almost). This recipe has the perfect balance of cherry to Nutella. It was an instant hit as soon as I made it. There is loads of potential to transform this cake into your own wonderful creation - your imagination is your only limit.

Method
'Bake the Secret way'.

Melt the dark/semi-sweet chocolate.

Mix the Nutella into the melted chocolate.

Separate the cheesecake mix by pouring 400g of it into a measuring jug and set aside.

Pour the melted chocolate Nutella mix into the large bowl of cheesecake mix and mix in thoroughly, ensuring no white cheese is visible. Pour onto the biscuit base.

Using only half of the remaining vanilla cheesecake, carefully pour a circle from the jug onto the top of the chocolate cheesecake, about an inch in from the edge.

It should look like a ring of vanilla on the top of the cake.

Mix the cherry flavoring and cherry food coloring into the remaining vanilla cheesecake in the jug.

This time pour directly onto the white vanilla ring you've just made.

Then gently push the brownies into the vanilla and cherry ring, so they disappear into the cheesecake mix. You want them to settle about halfway in the cheesecake.

Be careful not to touch the hot cheesecake!

Cool and chill.

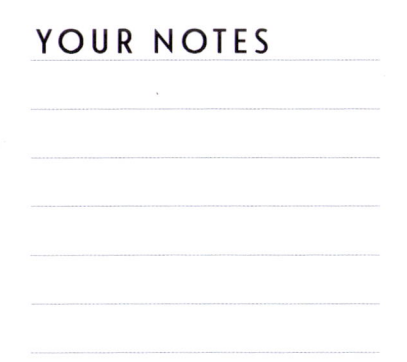

INSPIRATION

ALTERNATIVELY, YOU COULD CHANGE THE CHERRY FLAVOR TO RASPBERRY, MINT, ORANGE, OR EVEN ADD A LITTLE CARAMEL SAUCE, AND JUST CHANGE THE FOOD COLORING TO SUIT THE NEW FLAVOR AND, HEY PRESTO!

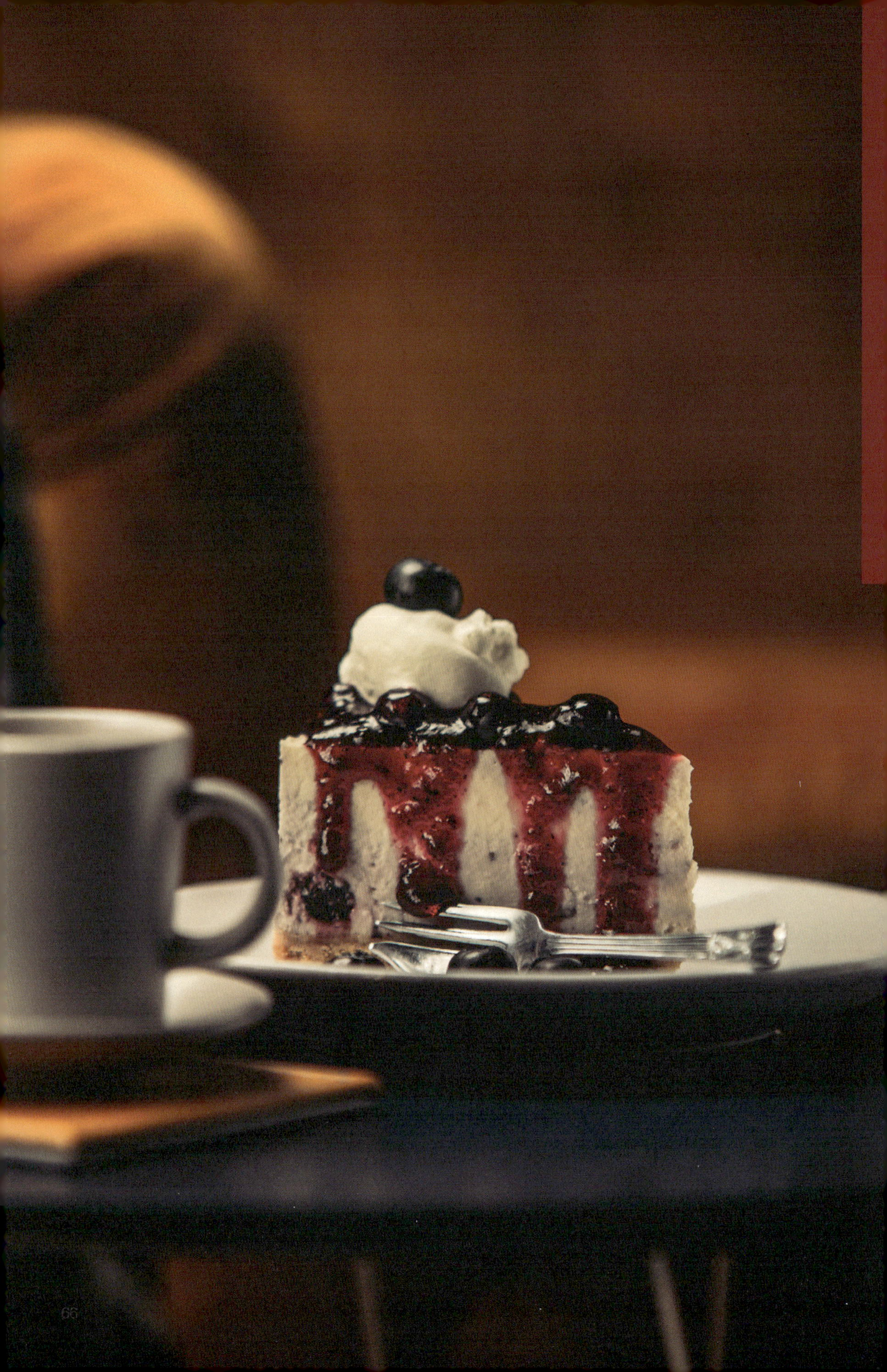

BLUEBERRY SWIRL

Swirling blueberry puree into creamy cheesecake batter not only creates a beautiful pattern but is exceedingly delicious. The blueberry cheesecake is the perfect mix of tartness and creaminess, refreshing and light, it's a perfect palate cleanser after a nice meal or served as a midday treat. A ginger biscuit base works really well.

Ingredients

300g good quality blueberry puree/jelly or jam

Method

Using the marbling method, mix the blueberries into half of the cheesecake mix.

Pour the cheesecake mix from a height of about 12 inches onto the biscuit base, creating the marble effect.

Cool and chill as usual.

YOUR NOTES

INSPIRATION

SWAP OUT THE BLUEBERRY FOR STRAWBERRY OR CHERRY, EXPERIMENT WITH YOUR FAVORITE FRUIT PUREE

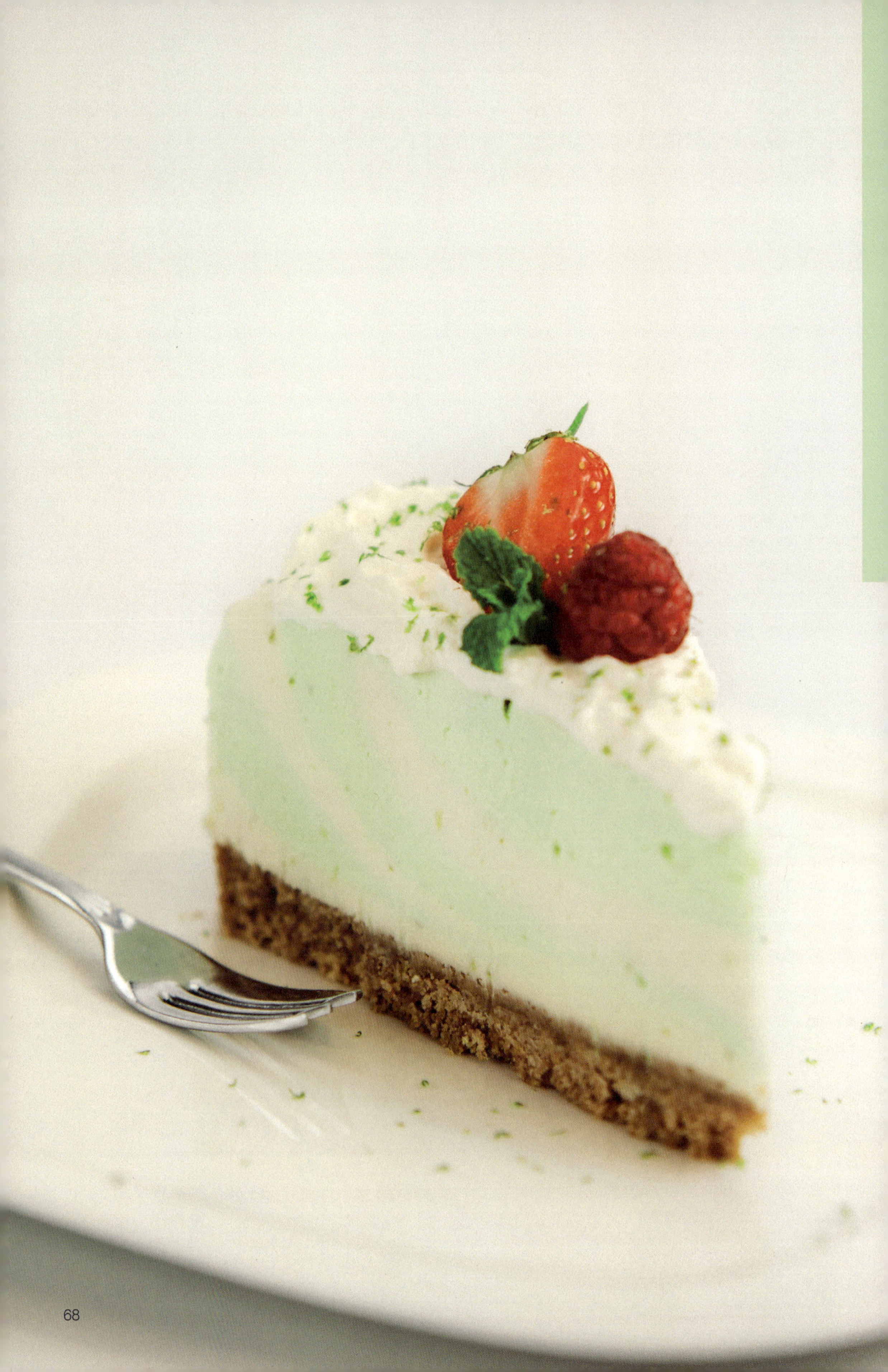

KEY LIME

Ingredients

The zest and juice of 3 limes
A couple of drops of green food coloring

The original Key Limes are from Malaysia and arrived in the Florida Keys in the 1500s, from where they got their name. Although we don't have easy access to real Key Limes in the UK, using three good quality limes still does the trick.

It's in the top 5 of my favorite flavors, best made with a ginger base, you could also use a digestive/Graham.

Method
Zest the limes straight into the bowl of unbaked cheesecake mix.

Squeeze in all the juice.

Because of the amount of liquid from the limes, we're going to add the zest and juice before we 'Bake the Secret way'.

Once the cheesecake mix is baked, add the food coloring and mix everything together.

Go steady with the food coloring because you only want to add a slight hint of green. Too much, and the cake will look radioactive.

YOUR NOTES

INSPIRATION

SWAP THE LIMES FOR LEMONS TO MAKE LEMON CHEESECAKE OR JUST ONE OF THE LIMES FOR A LEMON AND GO LEMON AND LIME FLAVOR!

THE BANOBLERONE?

People who love banoffee, LOVE Banoffee Pie Cheesecake. I like it, what's not to like? Vanilla cheesecake with bananas, caramel, and a chocolate biscuit pie crust!

"It's not my first choice, just not something I'd order from the menu", that's what I said to Gary and Adam, the two photographers, while we were on the photoshoot for the book.

As they were both deep in conversation, obsessing about the exact lighting for a slice of cheesecake, I felt slightly hungry, and it was nearly lunchtime anyway.

To my right was the Banoffee Pie cheesecake we'd just shot. "Hmm, I'll just try a bit", I thought to myself, as I rarely eat any Banoffee. "I'll make sure it tastes okay for everyone who buys the book's benefit".

It was the least I could do.

Wow! It tasted incredible! The rich vanilla cheesecake with the sweet banana, the hint of caramel, and the crunch of the chocolate biscuit! I was completely sold! I owe an apology to all the Banoffee addicts, who I thought were clearly misguided in their choice of desserts. They had it right all along.

As soon as I finished my unplanned sweet, creamy, delicious yet early lunch, Gary and Adam noticed I had just been eating something. So they made their way over to me, where I was still staring in disbelief at my empty plate and an almost full Banoffee cheesecake.

I looked at them both and told them, "You have to try it", and explained my previous lack of enthusiasm for it and now how I have, along with the cheesecake, eaten my words.

They both loved it and commented on how I could possibly have thought this was anything other than "one of the best cheesecakes they'd ever eaten". They named it "The Banoblerone" as the one in the shoot was piled high with Toblerone.

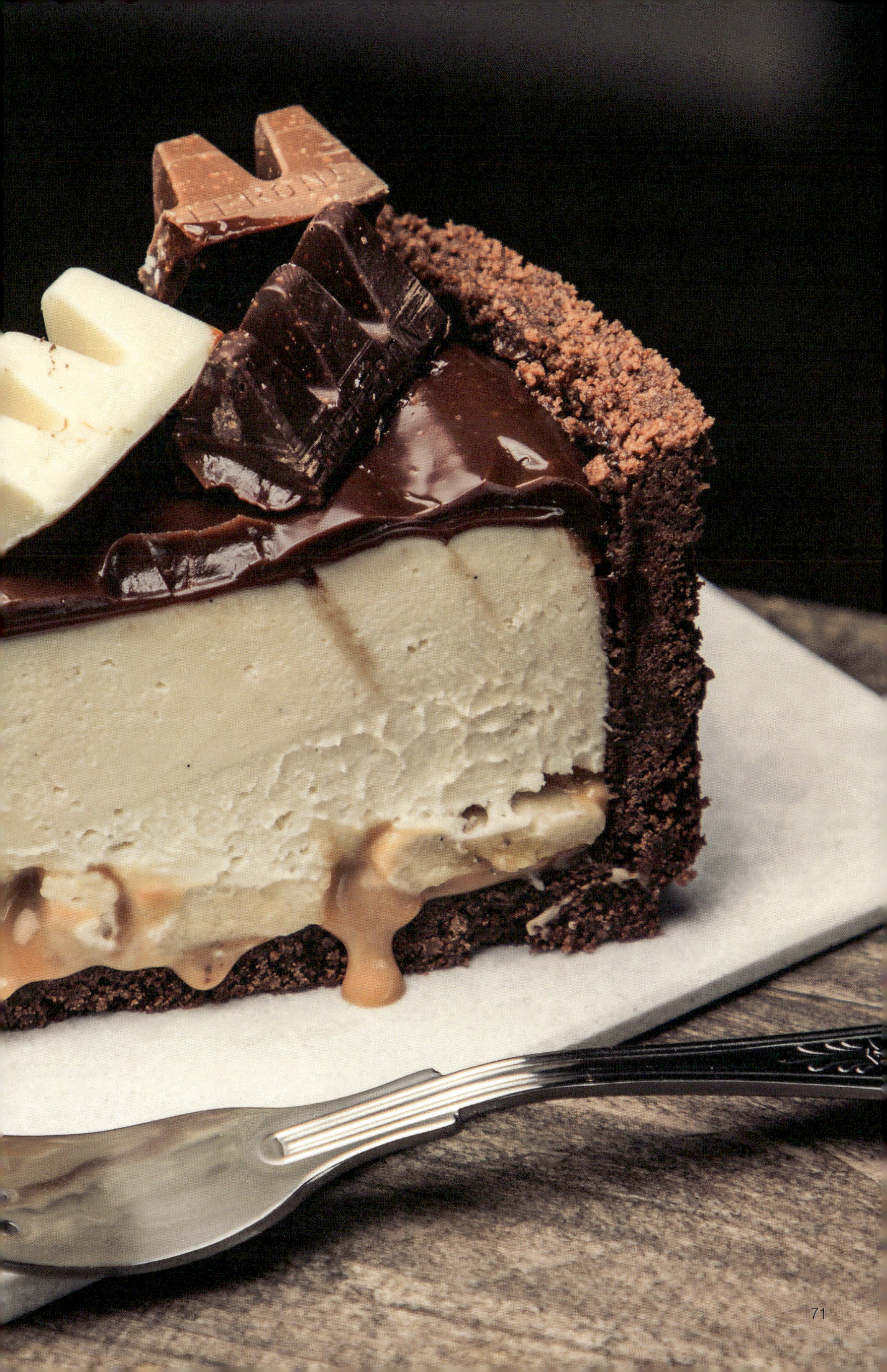

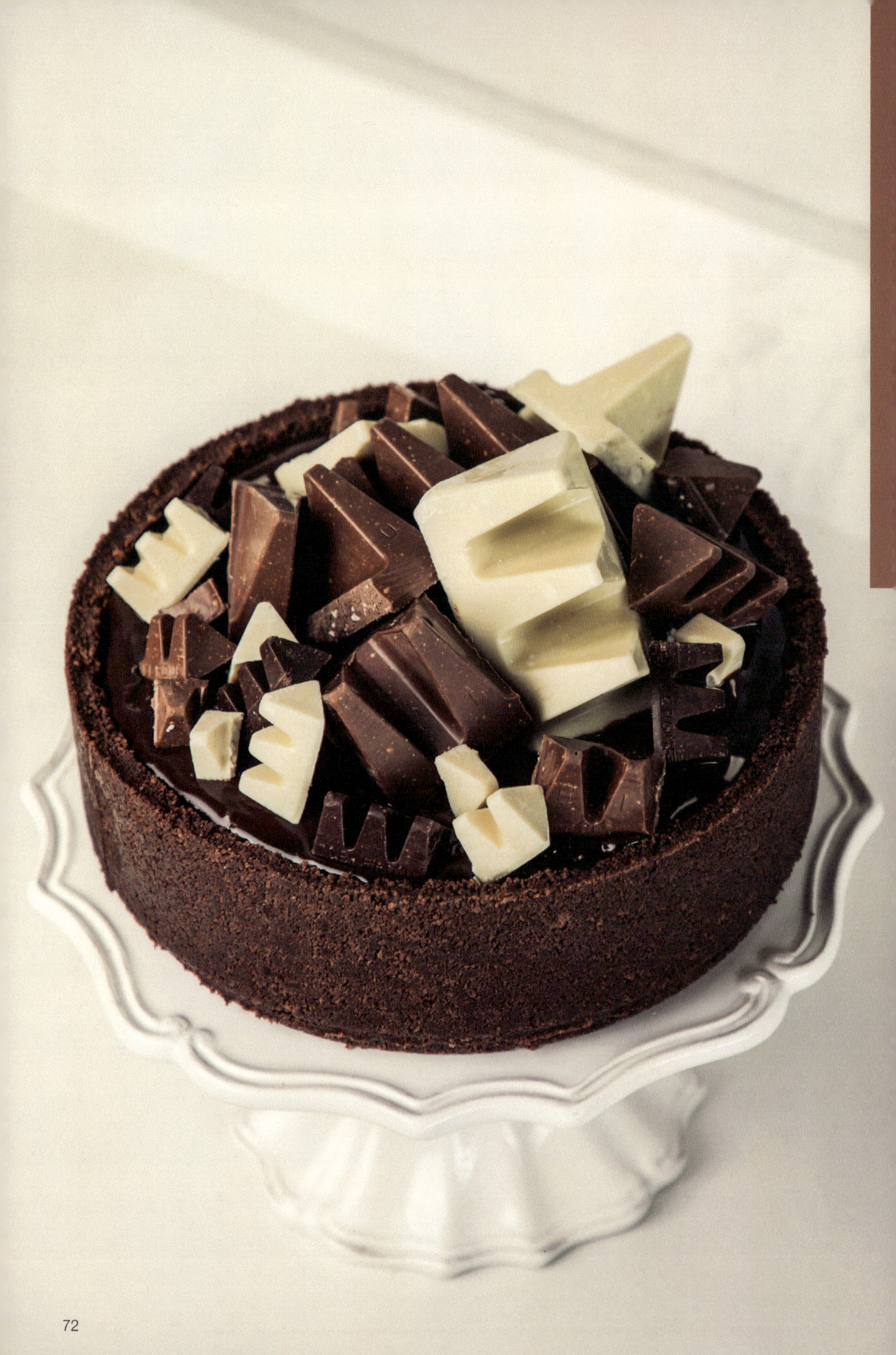

BANOFFEE PIE
(and eating my words)

Ingredients

One prepared biscuit pie crust
Vanilla cheesecake mix
2 medium bananas, sliced (approx. ½ inch/1cm)
150 g Dulce de leche caramel

There's been a debate in the cheesecake world (and yes, it's a real place) for some time about whether a cheesecake is a cake or a pie. The original cheesecakes did have a deep edge like a pie and so were called cheesecake pies. Fair enough.

So, in order not to offend anyone, I've opted to go with calling this a cheesecake pie.

The cheesecake pie collective and the cheesecakers can temporarily forget about their differences and unite over their love of delicious, sweet, baked cheesecake.

Method

Separate 800g of the baked 'cheesecake mix' into a separate bowl and mix it together with the Dulce de leche, you can leave a few lumps of caramel in it. These look great as they slowly ooze out of the bottom of the slice.

Arrange the bananas neatly on the biscuit base.

Pour the caramel cheesecake mix into the biscuit pie crust over the banana slices. Use a spatula if you need to even it out, or give it a gentle shake on the worktop.

Carefully pour the remaining vanilla cheesecake mix on top of the caramel cheese mix until it reaches the top of the biscuit wall.

Smooth over with a spatula.

Cool and chill as usual.

YOUR NOTES

INSPIRATION

NO MODIFICATIONS HERE. THE PURISTS WOULD HUNT ME DOWN

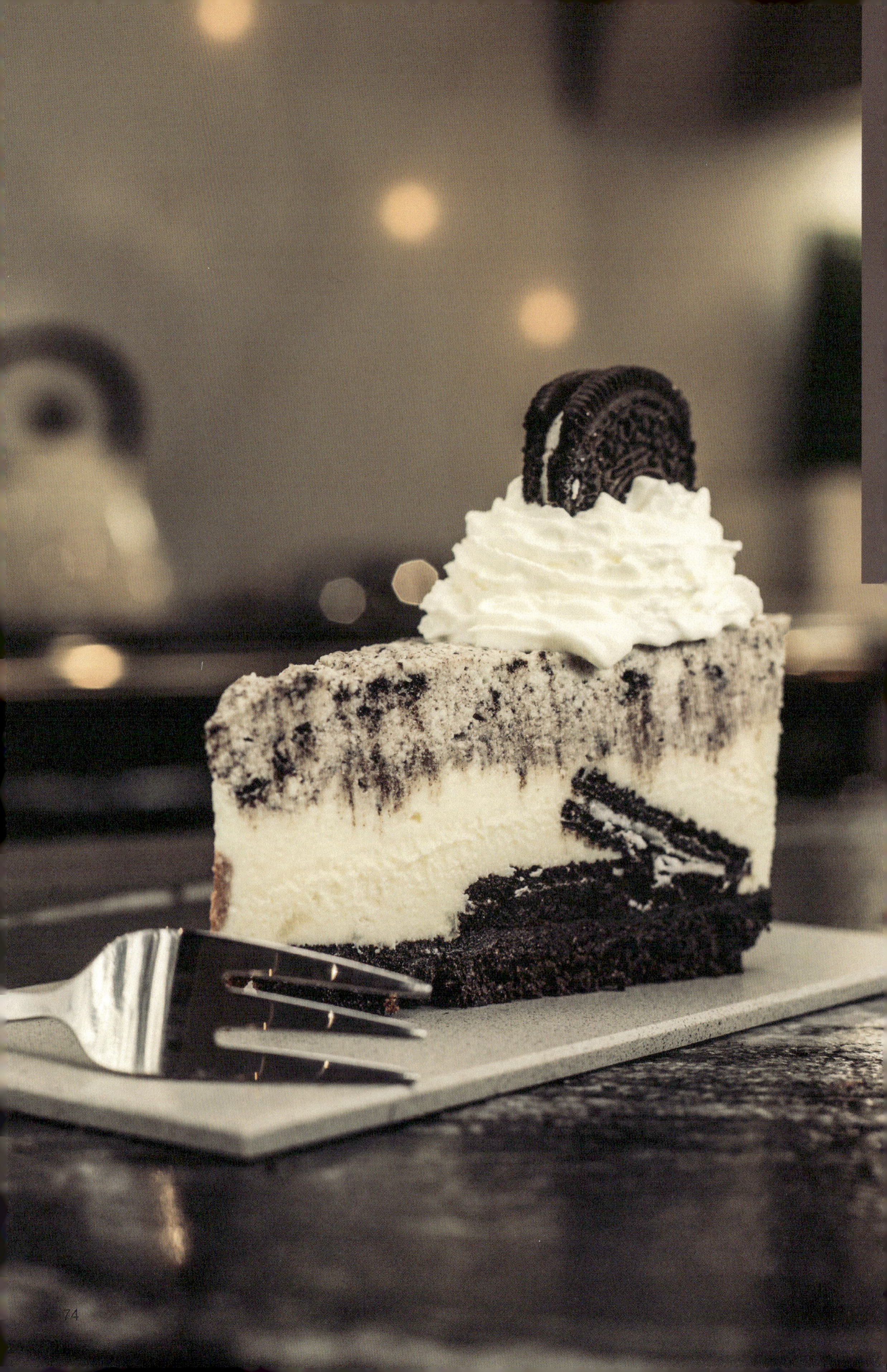

THE OREO

Ingredients

250g Oreos
100g white chocolate

I initially couldn't understand what all the fuss was about with Oreos. They were nice, but nothing exceptional. Then I had some Oreo ice cream, and everything made sense. By themselves, they are okay, but when used for flavoring other things, e.g. ice cream, milkshakes, brownies, and of course cheesecake, they are on another level.

We've sold Oreo brownie and blondie sundaes, milkshakes, and cheesecakes by the boatload at Cheesecake Geek. There was no way I could leave this one out.

Method
Melt the white chocolate.

Break up 100g of Oreos in a food processor or a resealable plastic bag with a rolling pin or something heavy until they are in crumbs. Don't worry if there are some bigger pieces than others, it doesn't have to be uniform.

Place the remaining Oreos onto the prepared Oreo biscuit base creating a ring of Oreos about an inch from the side of the cake tin.

Add more Oreos, and this time lean them on the first ring of Oreos.

Separate 800g of the baked cheesecake mix into another bowl and mix in the Oreo crumbs until they are evenly combined.

Pour the melted white chocolate into the remaining cheesecake mixture and mix well.

Carefully pour the white chocolate cheesecake mix into the cake tin over the Oreos you placed there earlier.

Pour the Oreo cheesecake mix over the white chocolate cheesecake mix carefully, and smooth over.

YOUR NOTES

INSPIRATION

ADD SOME MINT OR ORANGE EXTRACT, CARAMEL, OR MELT CHOCOLATE TO RECREATE YOUR FAVORITE OREO FLAVORS, OR EVEN BETTER, CREATE NEW FLAVORS

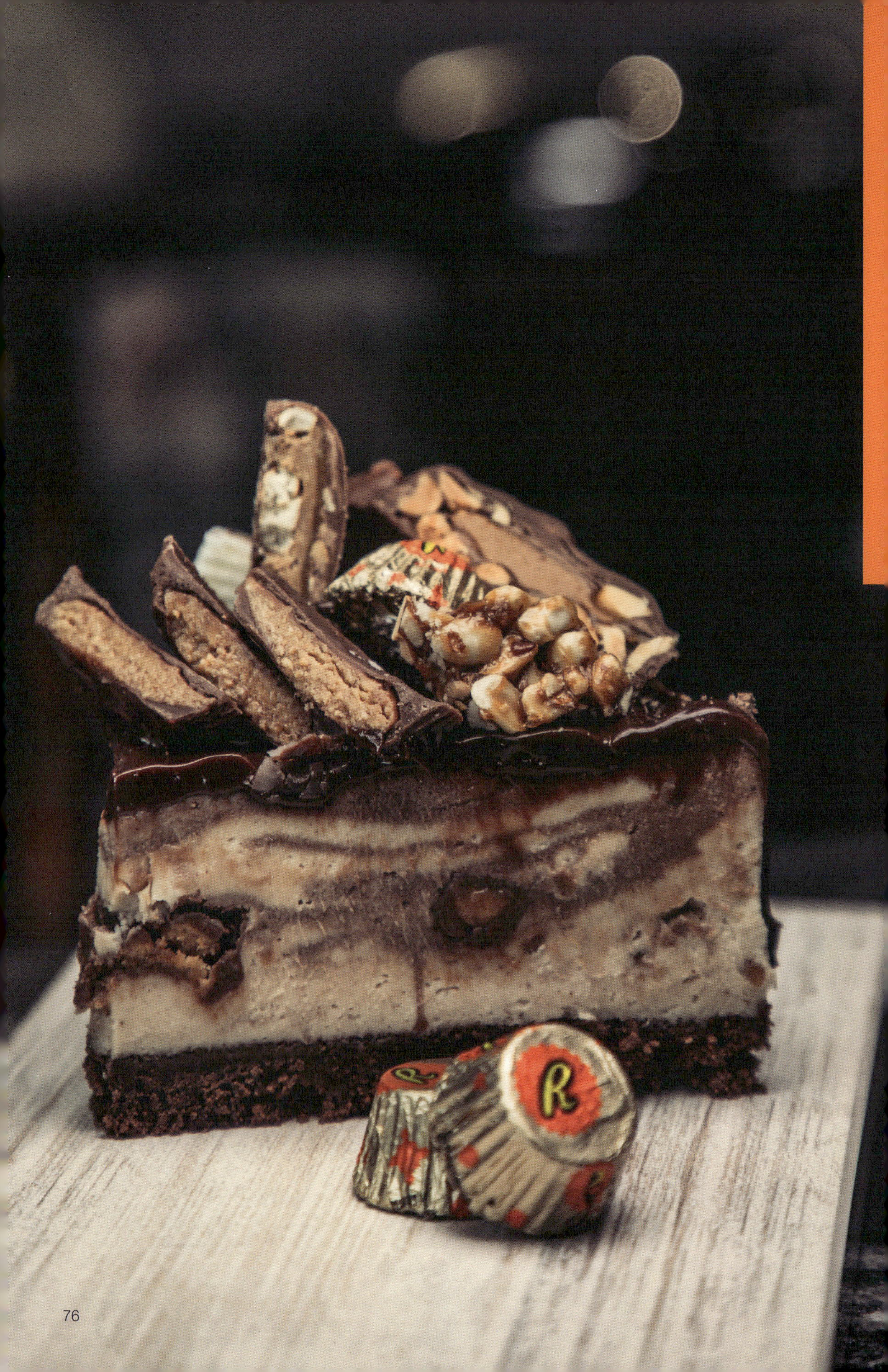

REESE'S PEANUT BUTTER CUP

Ingredients

200 g peanut butter (I prefer crunchy)
150 g Reese's Cups chopped
50 g milk chocolate
50 g dark chocolate

Thank you, America! I can't begin to tell you how much I love Reese's, as it's probably the best chocolate treat ever created.

You're most likely aware by now that almost anything can go into a cheesecake, and peanut butter is no exception. Reese's must be one of my favorite flavors. I'm a big peanut butter fan and therefore, a Reese's fan. The peanut butter also creates a wonderful texture in the cheesecake.

Decorate it with Reese's Krispy Kremes, Reese's cups, and peanut brittle. Your guests will love you.

Method

Mix the peanut butter into the baked cheesecake mix until it's all evenly combined.

Melt the chocolate together in a measuring jug.

Pour the chocolate into one side of the cheesecake mix, and using the marbling effect, mix it in carefully so that about a ¼ of the cooked mix is now chocolate.

Then add the chopped Reese's Cups into the ¾ peanut butter side and carefully fold them in.

Pour the mix into the prepared cake tin.

The cheesecake will have Reese's Cups mixed throughout the peanut butter cheesecake and have a beautiful chocolate marble swirl

YOUR NOTES

INSPIRATION

SWAP THE MILK CHOCOLATE FOR WHITE CHOCOLATE. IF YOU'VE NEVER TRIED WHITE CHOCOLATE AND PEANUT BUTTER, PREPARE TO HAVE YOUR MIND BLOWN

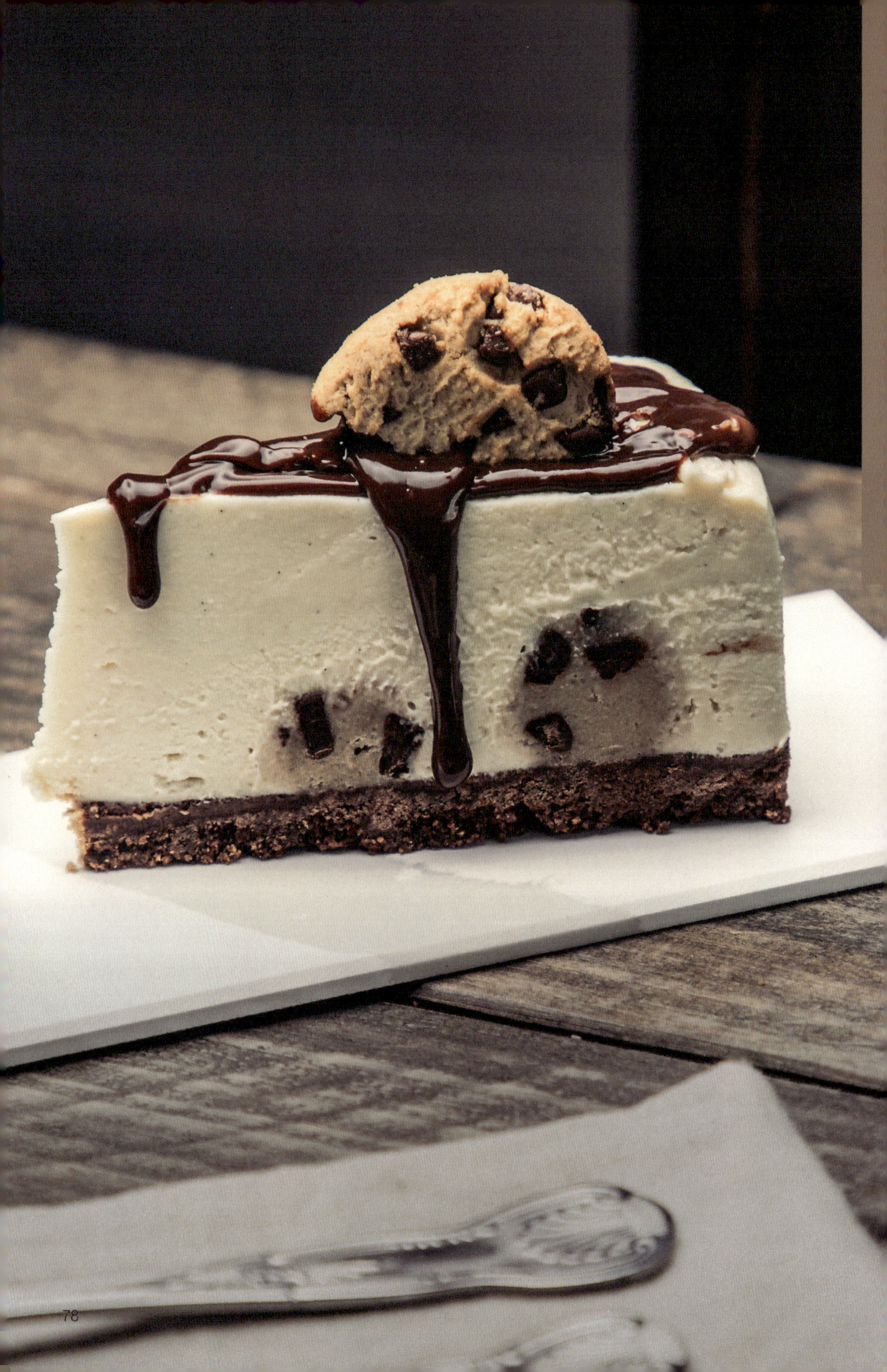

COOKIE DOUGH

Ingredients

600g cookie dough (chilled).
50g chocolate chips.
1 tbsp vanilla extract/paste.

Cookie dough wasn't 'a thing' when I was growing up in the UK in the 1980s. That was probably good, it's far too nice. Amazing on its own, cookie dough is the perfect addition to any self-respecting cheesecake. Creamy vanilla cheesecake with chunks of chocolate chip cookie dough, how could it not be nice?

When I originally made this, I used to make the cookie dough into small balls and fold them into the cheesecake mix, but because the amazing sweet balls of goodness were floating randomly in the cheesecake, occasionally some poor soul would get that one slice where there was no (or very little) cookie dough.

So, to resolve a potential catastrophe and possibly losing a friend, I started arranging the cookie dough in rings, a larger outer ring and a slightly smaller inner ring. Doing it this way means everyone will get the same amount of cookie dough in their slice and every slice will look like the perfect slice of cookie dough cheesecake.

Method
Stir in the vanilla.

Roll out the cookie dough into two long sausage shapes, one slightly longer and thicker than the other.

Arrange the longer piece on the outer edge of the cake tin and the shorter one on the inside of the larger ring

Note: make sure there's a gap between the tin and both pieces of cookie dough.

Now sprinkle the chocolate chips into the mix and quickly but carefully fold them in. Don't stir them too much as we don't want them to melt into the mixture.

Pour the mix into the prepared base.

Cool and chill as usual.

YOUR NOTES

INSPIRATION

ADD LARGE RAINBOW SPRINKLES AND M&M'S INSTEAD OF CHOCOLATE CHIPS TO THE COOKIE DOUGH AND FOLD MORE INTO THE CHEESECAKE

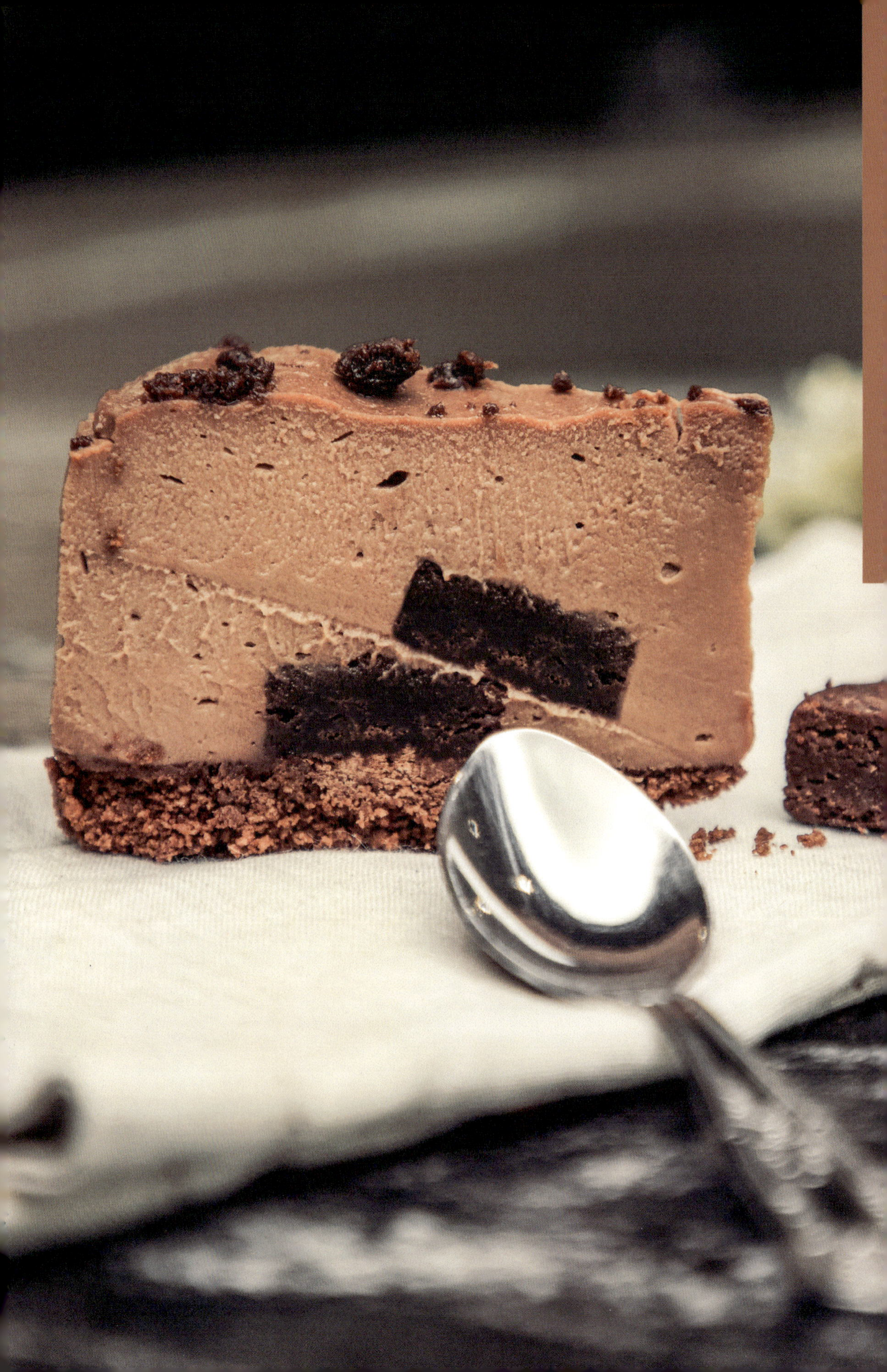

CHOCOLATE FUDGE BROWNIE

Ingredients

150g milk chocolate
150g dark chocolate
450g good quality brownies

A chocolate cheesecake with chocolate brownie pieces is a real chocolate lover's cheesecake. Rich and creamy chocolate cheesecake with the amazingly decadent fudgy chocolate brownies. Chocolate overload, if there is such a thing.

Method

Melt the chocolate and mix it thoroughly into the baked cheesecake mix and then fold in the brownies.

Pour it all into the prepared cake tin, cool, and chill as normal.

INSPIRATION

SEPARATE THE CHEESECAKE MIX EVENLY INTO TWO BOWLS

IN ONE HALF, MAKE UP THE COOKIE DOUGH MIX, AND IN THE OTHER, THE CHOCOLATE FUDGE BROWNIE MIX.

… BOOM!

THANK ME LATER…

YOUR NOTES

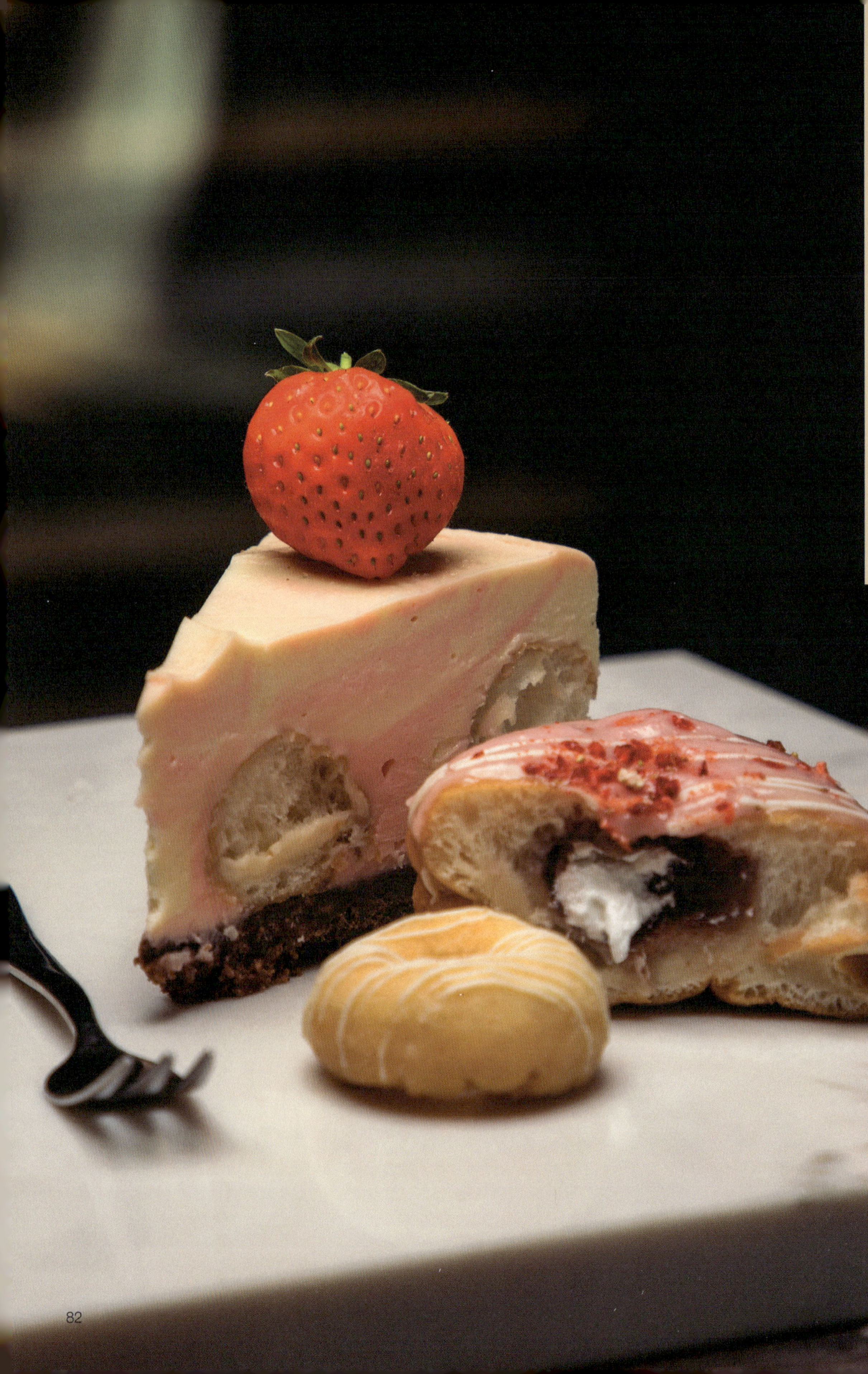

WHITE CHOCOLATE KRISPY KREME

Ingredients

4 Krispy Kreme donuts
200 g good white chocolate
A few drops of pink food coloring (or your favorite color)

An equally spectacular-looking and delicious cheesecake is the marriage of white chocolate cheesecake and Krispy Kreme donuts. They were meant to be love at first sight (I'm welling up thinking about it, just give me a minute).

Imagine, four sweet soft rings of pure joy floating in creamy white chocolate magnificence. I made this for the cast of Emmerdale when I had the pleasure of meeting them on set. For those of you who don't know what Emmerdale is, it's one of Britain's most popular soap operas, something like Dallas or Dynasty but set in a field in Yorkshire, in the north of England.

Method

Melt the white chocolate and mix it into the cheesecake mix.

'Bake using the Secret method'.

Add the pink food coloring into the edge of the bowl and mix it in carefully to a small patch using the marbling effect.

Place the donuts on the biscuit base in the prepared cake tin.

Pour the white chocolate cheesecake mix over the donuts from a height of 12 inches, making sure the mix gets into the donut holes.

Smooth over with the spatula.

Cool and chill as usual.

YOUR NOTES

INSPIRATION

I'VE OFTEN USED BELGIAN WAFFLES IN MY CHEESECAKES. THEY WORK VERY WELL. SWAP THEM FOR THE KRISPY KREMES, IT'S THAT EASY

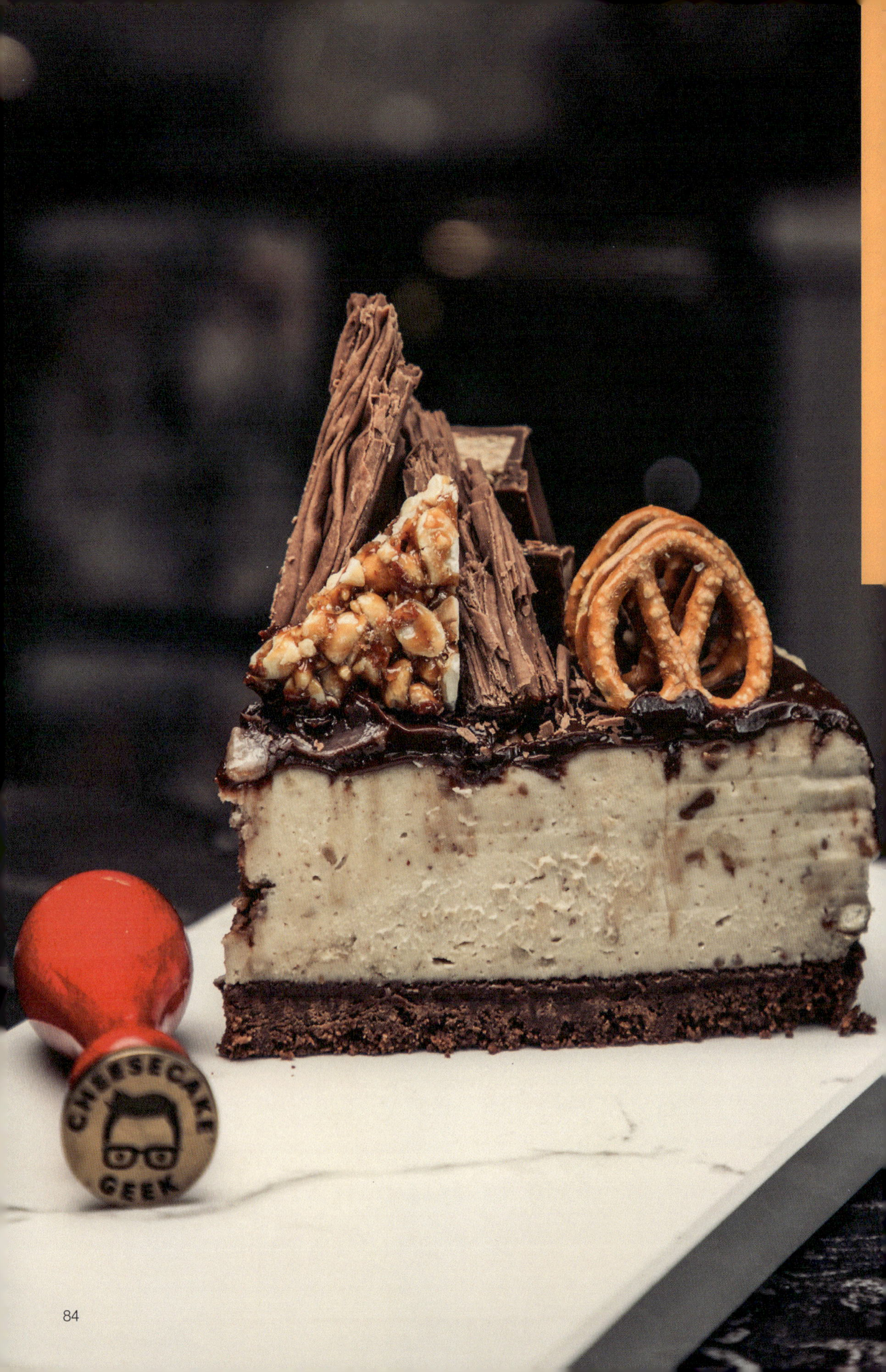
CHEESECAKE
GEEK

NETFLIX AND CHILLL'D

Ben and Jerry's inspired "Peanut butter with brownies and a sweet and salty pretzel swirl"

Ingredients
200g peanut butter
200g brownies (chopped into small 1cm/1/2-inch cubes)
50g pretzels (broken into small pieces)
1 tsp salt
1 tbsp sugar

No prizes for guessing what I was doing when I came up with this idea. Ice cream flavors are perfect for cheesecake flavors. Peanut butter cheesecake with sweet & salty pretzel swirls & brownie pieces, what's not to love? The whole Ben and Jerry's range can be transformed into their equivalent cheesecakes, cookie dough, chocolate brownie, etc.

This is exactly what I'm talking about when I say use your imagination, always be on the lookout for new and interesting flavor combinations.

Method

Mix the peanut butter into the baked cheesecake mix until it's all evenly combined.

Add the broken pretzels to a small corner of the bowl.

Pour the sugar and salt onto the pretzels.

Stir the pretzels gently as if you're creating a marble effect (that's what we're going to do with them).

Add the brownies.

Fold the pretzels and brownies into the mix a couple of times.

Pour the mixture into the prepared cake tin from 12 inches.

Decorating tip:

Pile up a few brownies on the side of the cake tin and lean some pretzels against the inside of the tin before you add the mixture.

YOUR NOTES

INSPIRATION

CHANGE THE PEANUT BUTTER, TO ALMOND OR PISTACHIO BUTTER?

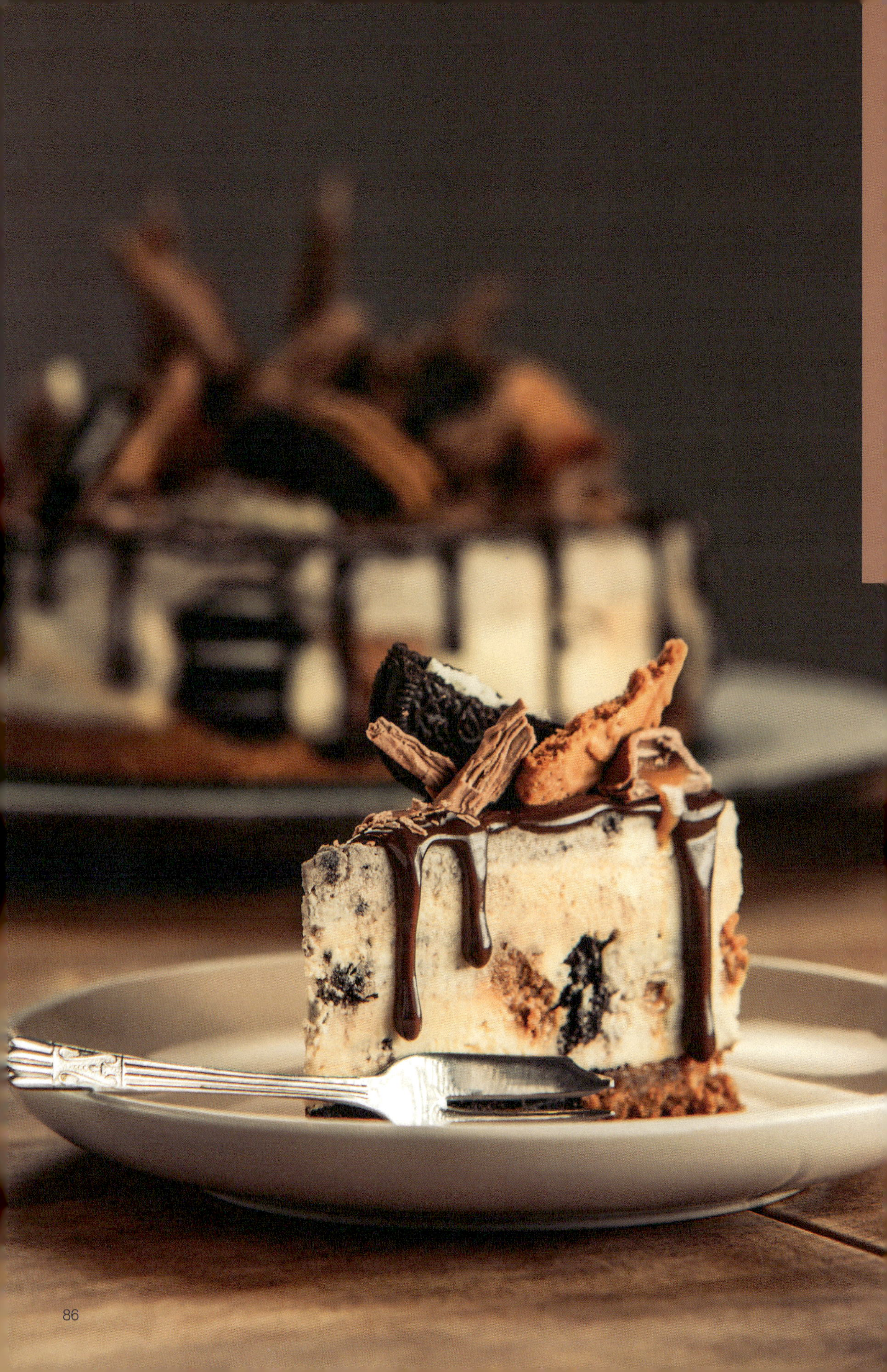

THE INCREDIBLE OREO AND BISCOFF SWIRL

Ingredients

100g Oreos crushed
100g Biscoff spread or crushed biscuits

At the time of writing this book, the Oreo Biscoff swirl was by far the most popular cheesecake I was being asked to make. The flavors are incredible together. With half Oreo and half Biscoff crust, it looks fantastic, I had to add it.

This is a perfect example of how to mix different flavors and colors.

Method

Using the marbling effect mix the crushed Oreos into one half of the baked cheesecake mix.

Carefully mix the crushed Biscoff into the other half of the bowl

You will now have half of the bowl Oreo and half Biscoff cheesecake mix.

Gently pour the mix from a height of about 12 inches onto the biscuit base, creating the marble effect.

Cool and chill as usual.

YOUR NOTES

INSPIRATION

WHAT ARE YOUR FAVORITE COOKIES?
WHAT DO YOU THINK WILL WORK WELL TOGETHER?
JUST SWAP THE OREO AND BISCOFF, AND MAKE SOMETHING BEAUTIFUL!

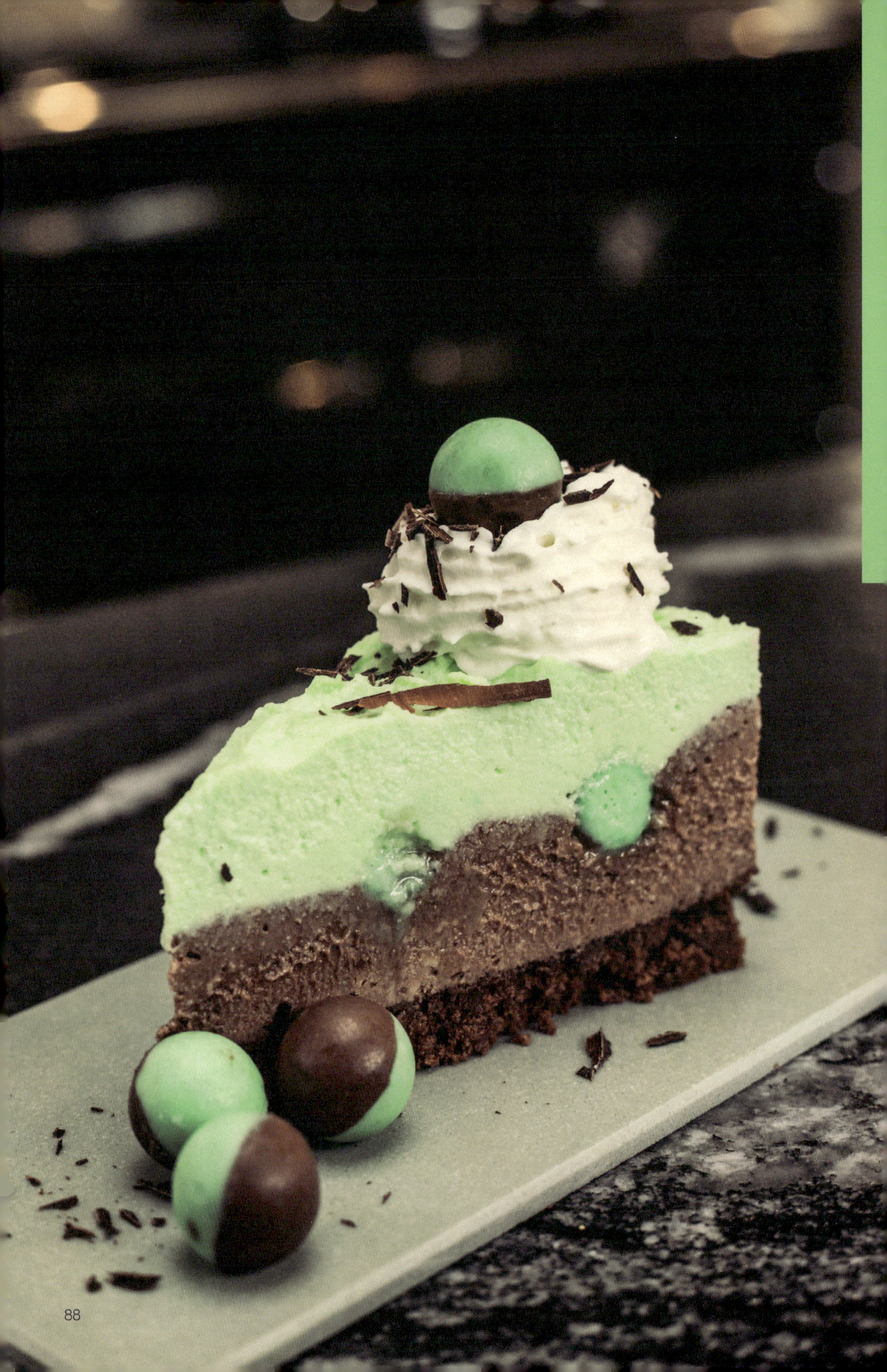

CHOCOLATE MINT

Ingredients

75 g dark/semi-sweet chocolate
75 g milk chocolate
1.5 tablespoons mint extract
A few drops of green food coloring

The nostalgic taste of chocolate mint is global. The smell brings back memories of devouring mouthfuls of it as a child, just like chocolate orange!

Which do you prefer? Chocolate mint or chocolate orange? It's a difficult choice as both work so well together. I've included both here because it's only a case of adding the different extracts.

I always use a mix of half milk and half dark/semi-sweet chocolate when making a chocolate cheesecake. Using milk chocolate alone doesn't leave a strong chocolate taste, so 50/50 is perfect, but if you're a big chocoholic, you can use all dark chocolate. Or even white chocolate. You're the Boss.

For this recipe, I've made a variation and created a chocolate and mint layer.

Method

Melt dark and milk chocolate together.

Add the mint extract to the baked cheesecake mix and stir well.

Separate the baked mix evenly into two bowls.

Mix the melted chocolate into one bowl and the green food coloring into the other.

Do not leave any white cheesecake mix showing.

Pour the chocolate mix into the prepared cake tin then carefully pour the green mix on top of the chocolate.

Cool and chill as usual.

YOUR NOTES

INSPIRATION

IT IS EASY TO TRANSFORM THIS INTO AN ELEGANT MOCHA CHEESECAKE, BY ADDING TWO SHOTS OF STRONG ESPRESSO OR DISSOLVING TWO TABLESPOONS (OR TO TASTE) OF YOUR FAVORITE INSTANT COFFEE INTO THE HEAVY/DOUBLE CREAM BEFORE YOU ADD IT TO THE CHEESECAKE MIX

#MYCHEESECAKEGEEK

YOUR RECIPE!

Your ingredients

_____

_____

_____

I've added this page just for you, so you can add your own amazing cheesecake creation.

Design and create your own unique cheesecake using all your favorite flavors, and colors.

Write your method here

_____
_____
_____
_____
_____
_____
_____
_____
_____
_____

YOUR NOTES

_____

_____

_____

_____

INSPIRATION

PLEASE SHARE YOUR NEW CREATION AND INSPIRE OTHERS.

POST IT IN THE CHEESECAKE GEEK WORLD GROUP ON FACEBOOK OR ON INSTAGRAM USING #MYCHESSECAKEGEEK

CONCLUSION

You have now been initiated into the Cheesecake Geek Book of Secrets.

Who you share these secrets with is up to you. I'd like to think they would get handed down to each generation, from parents to children.

As wonderful as sharing is, it's also nice to have a little 'air of mystery with some of your cooking'. This book and its methods fall directly into that category.

Your unique cheesecakes will arouse excitement, curiosity, and suspense because of an unknown, obscure and enigmatic quality that is known only to you.

Be prepared to be asked, "Will you be bringing one of your famous cheesecakes?" to every family event.

THANK YOU

If this book has helped you in anyway, I would really appreciate it if you could leave a review on Amazon.

Not only will it help others to find this book and join our amazing Cheesecake Geek community, but I also read every single comment and will incorporate your feedback into future book projects.

Once again a big thank you for purchasing this book, it means so much to me, and I can't wait to see your amazing creations. Don't forget to post them into Cheesecake Geek World Facebook group and on Instagram. Tag them with #mycheesecakegeek so I and others can see your beautiful creations.

Jaime

CHEESECAKE GEEK
JAIME FIRBANK

REINVENTING CHEESECAKE